MAINSTREAM SPORT

LIVERPOOL'S DREAM TEAM

STAN HEY

MAINSTREAM
PUBLISHING

EDINBURGH AND LONDON

First published in Great Britain in 1997 by
MAINSTREAM PUBLISHING COMPANY (EDINBURGH) LTD
7 Albany Street
Edinburgh EH1 3UG

ISBN 1 84018 681 X

This edition, 2002

A catalogue record for this book is available from the British Library

Typeset in Garamond
Printed and bound in Great Britain by
Cox & Wyman Ltd

For my dad then; for Charlie and Jack now

Contents

Acknowledgements

I would like to thank the following people who were of enormous help to me in the writing of this book. First and foremost, I'm grateful to all the Liverpool players who gave up their time to talk to me, and I hope that they won't feel it was wasted when they read the book. Only Kenny Dalglish, reluctantly, declined to be interviewed on the grounds that he and his publishers did not want anything to clash with his highly successful autobiography. As if. Many people helped me contact the players, or jogged my memory, or provided new information. So I'm grateful to Dick Barton, my brother Keith Hey, Phil Shaw of *The Independent*, Ian Ross of *The Guardian*, Steve Tongue of Radio 5 Live!, Terry Lawler, Jon Holmes and Diana van Bunnens of Park Associates, Judith Horey of Newcastle United and Brian Hall and the Public Relations Office at Liverpool FC. A special thanks to Gary Lineker for his contributions. The book would not have been possible without reference to Brian Pead's *Liverpool: a Complete Record*, an easy choice as my Desert Island book. I'd also like to thank Judy Diamond for putting up with my late arrival in the penalty area, and my agent Cat Ledger who secured me the contract – bung-free, of course. Finally, a personal word of thanks to my wife Wendy who has had to live with my collection of old Liverpool programmes for the last year. I promise I'll take them off the dinner table soon.

Introduction

If you grew up in Liverpool in the 1950s, football was not a leisure activity which you could choose to ignore.

It was on the doorstep with the milk-bottles and the orange squash, it was probably in the dolly mixtures they gave you at the clinic after your polio injections, it was in the songs of the school playground, and it was in the church or Sunday school which you attended. Indeed the vestiges of Merseyside sectarianism usually affected your choice between Everton and Liverpool, between blue and red, between Catholic and Protestant.

As the child of a Protestant father and a Catholic mother, I could have gone either way, except for the fact that my mother didn't really take an interest in football until she fell for Eusebio and his antics in the 1966 World Cup. By then, my dad's influence had already taken effect. He was a Red through and through and had even been to the Cup final in 1950, less than a year before he married my mum in March 1951. So from the time I could understand these things I was a Liverpool supporter by birth, waiting only for the baptismal rite of attending a game.

The Reds had been relegated to Division Two in 1954 and from what I can remember of my first infant school in Maidford Road, Dovecot, Everton fans outnumbered Reds by about two to one. Everton were still in the First Division, and Liverpool were definitely the underdogs, a fact which made them even more appealing to me. I always supported the Indians against the Cowboys for the same reason.

While Liverpool were still able to boast of the talent of Scottish international winger Billy Liddell, whose shots were reported by my dad as having 'burst the back of the net', the club looked doomed to a prolonged spell of frustration in the Second Division and they continued to miss out on promotion back to Division One – third in 1956 and 1957, fourth in 1958 and 1959, and third again in 1960 and 1961.

During this time I was only allowed to go with my dad to Saturday afternoon reserve games, which used to kick off early to save the expense of putting on the floodlights. The small, usually moaning crowds added to the general atmosphere of torpor and decay. I remember standing at the back of the Anfield Road terrace boxed in by corrugated metal sheeting which all of us youngsters would back-heel in rhythm to set up the treble-voiced, three-syllable chants of 'Liv-er-pool!' to no great effect on the team of stiffs.

In 1958 we had moved from our 'corpy house' in Newenham Crescent about half a mile down Pilch Lane to a post-war semi in Swanside Road, bought with a mortgage of £1,500. Our 'upward mobility' was marked for me by the fact that a first-team Liverpool footballer, Jimmy Harrower, also lived in the street and could be glimpsed some mornings walking to the number 75 bus stop, from where he would travel to Liverpool's training ground at Melwood in the suburb of West Derby.

This excitement was offset by the fact that I was forced to change schools, our half-mile move having crossed the invisible boundary between Liverpool's Education Committee and Lancashire's, leaving friends of two years' standing behind, and joining Malvern County Junior School as a complete stranger. For what seemed like an eternity I had no friends, until my nan bought me a bag of marbles for schoolyard games and my mum ran up a Liverpool kit to establish my allegiance. There were no such things as replica kits in those days, but you could get a cloth 'Liver Bird' badge from one of the drapery shops in town and stitch it onto the chest of a V-necked, short-sleeved red shirt with white cuffs and neck, while two strips of red ribbon would do for the stripes on the white shorts. Boots were terrible clumping affairs with big round toes and wooden studs tacked onto – and sometimes through – the soles with half-inch nails. And, worst of all, they had custard-yellow laces.

But the kit and, to a lesser extent, the marbles at least broke the ice with the others kids as the dinner-time and after-school kick-about teams were selected entirely on red v blue lines. One boy who used to sport Wolverhampton Wanderers' colours was always put in goal as a penance. Friends like Peter Donnelly, Phil Edge, the 'Two Robbos' – Dave and Pete – and Peter Snowdon gradually emerged to form a red cluster in our year, and we began to go to reserve games and Liverpool Schoolboys fixtures at Anfield as an innocently unsupervised group.

This social progress reached giddying heights when we went as a gang to a first-team home game, standing in the Boys' Pen, a sixpence-a-head, barred enclosure high up on the left flank of the Kop. The joke at the time was that the bars were there to protect the Kop from the Boys' Pen, and the memories of the games glimpsed from it – you couldn't actually see much of the pitch – are swamped by images of intimidation, under-age smoking, burning newspapers and the occasional scuffle.

But a chance happening produced the first definitive view of a Liverpool game. I had intercepted Jimmy Harrower one morning on his walk past our house and thrust a newly acquired autograph book upon him with a request for it to be passed around the dressing-room. Within a week of this Harrower had been trans-ferred, to Newcastle I think, and the autograph book was never returned.

Jack Rushton, a friend of my dad's at the English Electric factory where he worked, took pity on me and not only furnished me with a new book, signed by both the Liverpool and Everton squads of the time, but also with a stand ticket for a third-round FA Cup-tie at Anfield.

The date was Saturday, 6 January 1962, and the opponents were Chelsea whom Liverpool beat 4–3 in a thrilling game, with Liver-pool taking a 4–1 lead into half-time – one goal from Ian St John, two from Roger Hunt and one from Alan A'Court – but allowing Chelsea back into it the second half. I'd just turned ten years old, and seeing the Kop from the outside for the first time was a genuinely terrifying experience – there were 48,455 spectators that day, with about 28,000 of them packed onto the terrace, swaying just to stay on their feet. The cocktail of noise, goals and an underdog's victory almost felt as though it had been laid on specially for me.

From that moment on, there was no other club, no other faith even. When the team were promoted later that year I genuinely felt that my support had had something to do with it, but I suppose all ten-year-olds think the world revolves around them. In the next round of the Cup they played away at Oldham Athletic, but we were booked into a matinee of Ken Dodd's Christmas Show at the Royal Court. At about twenty minutes to five, Doddy was dancing around the stage wildly hitting a bass drum. He disappeared into the wings for a moment then returned, banging the drum in a more recognisable rhythm and singing:

> *Roses are Red, Violets are Blue*
> *Oldham one, Liverpool two!*

Doddy lived not far from us in Knotty Ash and was already a local hero. But as 1962 progressed, Doddy and the Liverpool team were joined by The Beatles in what seemed to be a modern alchemy, in which anything Liverpudlian turned into a national success. At the school's Christmas party, Peter Donnelly and I had already learnt the words to 'Love Me Do' and, by way of the group's live appearances on Granada's *Scene at Six-Thirty*, had clocked that Paul was left-handed while John was right-handed. Pity we couldn't sing though.

Liverpool's first season back in the top flight ended with a respectable eighth place – two draws against Everton, a win and a draw against Manchester United – but Everton won the title. Even worse was a traumatic FA Cup semi-final defeat to Leicester City at Hillsborough, which produced a collective groan around the cafeteria in Littlewoods' store where we were shopping when the result was broadcast. A photo showing Gordon Banks apparently laughing at a distraught Ian St John – it was no such thing, of course, just the effect of the angle – turned the England goalkeeper into a hate-

14

figure for a while, but his skills soon came to be appreciated, and I particularly remember Bill Shankly walking Banks around the pitch at Anfield after the car accident which had ended his career, orchestrating the ovation for one of the great goalkeepers of the modern age.

In August 1963, I moved into secondary education at Prescot Grammar School, a 30-minute bus ride on the number 10, but the journey seemed worth it because it was former Liverpool and England winger Alan A'Court's old school. The ex-Malvernians, together with other groups from junior schools around Huyton, formed the Scouse element to a school which also boasted local Prescotian kids and pure 'woolly-backs' from St Helens. To be identified as a Red, therefore, took on new significance in the presence of rugby league supporters, although I'd crossed the line a few times myself by going to watch the hopeless Liverpool City rugby league team at their decrepit Knotty Ash stadium.

Fortunately the school did not encourage rugby of either code, preferring football, hockey, cricket, athletics and tennis as its five major sports. The school football teams were of quite a high standard – the first XI regularly reached the final of the Merseyside Schools Shield, and often won it – but down in the lower forms it was still kick-and-run stuff. My own career was soon cut short by the sudden onset of short-sightedness at the age of 12 – no, not for the reason you might think – after which I was relegated to a select group of players christened, with punishing cruelty, as 'the leftovers'. But footballing ambition was in safer hands with the Reds.

In my first year at senior school, Liverpool finally shook off their mediocrity and won the league title for the first time since 1947. They clinched it with a fantastic 5–0 win over Arsenal on Saturday, 18 April 1964, a game I watched from the tumultuous, singing Kop, clinging to a crush barrier with one arm and saluting the goals with the other. Television cameras from *Panorama* were there to record the event, not just as a football achievement but also as a cultural phenomenon, for the swaying, chanting Kop had penetrated the circles of what would now be called the chattering classes.

When the programme went out a few weeks later, fronted by that

15

voice of the Establishment, Richard Dimbleby, it really did seem like a world-turning moment. The reporter John Morgan stood in front of the Kop as it sang its way through such contemporary anthems as 'She Loves You' and 'Anyone Who Had a Heart', mixed with contrapuntal chants of players' names – 'Rowdy Yeats!', 'St John!'.

Watching that programme on a video now, Morgan's prose seems hopelessly over the top and ever so slightly patronising, but then football was still regarded in those days as an activity played by, and on behalf of, the rough working class. Morgan talked of 'the gay and inventive ferocity' of the Kop, of how its rhythmic swaying 'was as rich and mystifying as any ritual on a South Sea island', and how it was 'in touch with Wacker, the spirit of Scouse'.

I suspect that the reality was something simpler – a collective euphoria generated by the Liverpool team's success after 17 blank seasons, allied to a vague but discernible sense of civic self-importance created by the success of so many Merseybeat groups. In the year from April 1963, Liverpool groups posted 12 Number One hits, including the one that would go on to be Liverpool's lasting anthem, 'You'll Never Walk Alone' by Gerry and the Pacemakers. The American beat poet Allen Ginsberg declared around this time that 'Liverpool is the centre of the known universe', and, believe me, it felt just like that, emphasised as it was in October 1964 by Huyton's Labour MP Harold Wilson kicking out the grouse-shooting Tory government.

No less memorable was 1965. The team produced a remarkable performance on its European début, beating the likes of Anderlecht (the début of the all-red strip) and Cologne to reach the semi-final of the European Cup and winning the FA Cup for the first time, by beating Leeds United 2–1 at Wembley in extra-time. I couldn't get a ticket for the FA Cup final, but went with the family into town on the Sunday to watch the trophy being paraded through the streets to the Town Hall. I can remember vividly that people danced on the roofs of buildings overlooking the parade, while we settled for a modest but appropriate spot outside the Leeds Building Society offices on Lord Street.

Determined not to miss out on another great event, two days later on Tuesday, 4 May, a gang of us went straight from school to watch the home leg of the European Cup semi-final against Inter Milan, who were the holders and reigning World Champions.

The streets around Anfield were bizarrely quiet at five o'clock when we arrived, but this was because the ground was already very nearly full, so keen was the anticipation for this match. One slight problem we encountered was that out school ties and caps were black and blue, the colours of Inter, and there were quite a few bewildered fans around us in the Anfield Road End who thought we were Italian schoolboys who'd sagged off from our studies in Milan – until the red-and-white scarves came out of our satchels.

The match was a major thrill. Inter Milan, or FC Internazionale as they were billed on the programme, boasted such talents as Mazzola, Suarez, Jair, Facchetti and Burgnich in their line-up, but they were totally unnerved by the Kop's singing. Bill Shankly had sent out the injured Gerry Byrne and Gordon Milne to parade the FA Cup around the ground, so there was already a triumphal atmosphere, but when the Inter team broke the established protocol by going to the Kop half of the field for their warm-up, they were shooed away by 28,000 Scouse voices, who were soon singing 'Go back to Italy' to the tune of 'Santa Lucia'.

Liverpool backed up the noise with their attacking football, with Roger Hunt slamming home a right-foot volley in the fourth minute and, although Inter equalised through Mazzola, Ian Callaghan scored from a brilliant free-kick move on 35 minutes, and Chris Lawler had a further goal mysteriously disallowed. In the second half Ian St John poked home a rebound off the goalie Sarti to give Liverpool a stunning 3–1 win, and apparent security.

It was almost impossible to believe that these foreign sophisticates in their white shirts with an exotic black-and-blue sash could be beaten by our humble team, but it was all true.

The second leg was unfortunately a different story, as Milan benefited from two extremely dodgy decisions by the referee – Peiro being allowed to kick the ball out of Tommy Lawrence's hands before scoring, then a direct shot from an indirect free-kick being judged as legal – to win the return leg 3–0. They went into the final which – surprise, surprise – was held in their own San Siro stadium.

But that disappointment was followed by another league title in the 1965–66 season, which included a famous 5–0 home win over Everton in September which was quickly enshrined in a chant – 'and we played the Toffees for a laugh, and left them feeling Blue, five-nil!' – and in May 1966 a narrow defeat by a jammy goal to Borussia Dortmund in the European Cup-Winners' Cup final at Hampden Park. Liverpool had beaten the likes of Juventus and Celtic *en route*, and though I was allowed to go to the Juventus game, my dad banned me from the Celtic match for fear of crowd trouble, which duly arrived when Geoff Strong headed the winner and a shower of green bottles – which I know now to be 'Bucky' tonic wine – flew out from the Glasgow hordes at the Anfield Road End.

But after the euphoria of England's World Cup triumph at Wembley, and our school trip to Austria that cleverly allowed us to see the great matches between Brazil, Hungary and Portugal at Goodison in the first phase, and still make it back home in time to see the final on television, I was judged, at 14 years of age, to be able to look after myself as far as going to football matches on my own was concerned.

So on the first day of the 1966–67 season, a sunlit Kop was in full voice, singing 'We All Live on a Red-and-White Kop' to the tune of the latest Beatles hit 'Yellow Submarine' as our bogey team Leicester City were beaten 3–2, and I was now a fully fledged Liverpool supporter.

Over the next five seasons, I barely missed a home game, and regularly travelled away to the likes of Burnley, Blackburn Rovers and the two Manchester clubs. A weekend job – first on the carwash and later on the petrol pumps – at Don Duncan's garage in Derby Lane, Old Swan, provided the pocket-money, with Mr Duncan ferrying me to Anfield every other Saturday afternoon in his black Humber Snipe, and then back to work at the garage afterwards.

Football merged with soul music, the latest mod fashions and going to Brooklands disco in Huyton as teenage passions, although the lingering smell of petrol tended to limit my chances at the disco on Saturday nights. Unfortunately at that time, Liverpool suddenly became a 'nearly' team after three heady seasons. In 1966–67 they were tonked 5–1 in the European Cup by an Ajax Amsterdam side sporting the young Johan Cruyff, and were beaten by an Alan Ball goal in the FA Cup fifth round by Everton, a game our gang watched on giant television screens at Anfield. Oh, and Manchester United won the league. In 1967–68 we signed the lumbering Tony Hateley as our new centre-forward, watched in horror as new boy Emlyn Hughes rugby-tackled a Stoke City player in his first game for the club, and lost to West Brom in a sixth-round FA Cup replay at Maine Road, leaving our little Vauxhall Viva's hub caps behind in Moss Side, an additional trophy for Manchester City who won the League.

In 1968–69, bastard Leicester City knocked us out of the Cup, an event made worse by Roger Hunt throwing his shirt onto the touchline right in front of me when he was substituted in the replay at Anfield, while bastard Leeds United won the League. We went out of the European Fairs Cup in the first round, losing to Athletic Bilbao on the toss of a coin. In 1969–70, lowly Watford knocked us out of the FA Cup, Vitoria Setubal beat us on away goals in Europe, we lost 4–1 at home to a Manchester United side with Law, Best and Charlton at the top of their form, and Everton, of all teams, won the league. Character-forming, or what?

The 1970–71 season was my last as a full-time Liverpool resident. I'd got four A-levels in the summer, despite (because of?) the distraction of watching the Mexico World Cup, and in September I was offered a place at St Catharine's College, Cambridge, to read English from October 1971. The rebuilt Liverpool team, with Tommy Smith as captain, Steve Heighway on the wing and Welsh international John Toshack up front, began to show signs of a revival, which was exemplified by a 3–2 home win over Everton after being two goals down. They also reached the semi-final of the Fairs Cup, where Leeds knocked us out thanks to a solitary Billy Bremner goal in the Anfield leg of the tie. Bremner celebrated his score by lying prostrate on the turf, giving a sly two-fingered salute to the Kop on the blind-side of the referee.

A gang of us went across to Leeds for the second leg on 28 April, travelling in a borrowed bread van which had had the shelving removed, but apart from a Steve Heighway volley which flew inches wide, Liverpool couldn't get themselves back into the game. As the van bucked its way back over the Pennines in the darkness, there was animated chat about whether Liverpool would ever win anything again, but there was still some optimism for the coming Cup final against Arsenal on 8 May. After all, we'd beaten Everton 2–1 in the semi-final at Old Trafford which seemed like a good omen.

The scramble for Wembley tickets was the usual mixture of false leads and wild-goose chasing. Since January I'd been working during the week as a filing clerk at the Liverpool City Planning Office (£13 per week), while also putting in a few hours on some evenings and weekends at the garage in order to save for my forthcoming student life. So, for once, money wasn't the problem. Finding somebody with a ticket to sell was, particularly as our sixth-form's Liverpool supporters' group had designated the match for a lads' reunion, with most of them having nearly completed their first year at university. Those studying in London, like Derek Proffitt at Imperial College, had already been notified that the floors of their rooms would be required for sleeping purposes.

In the end, I got a ticket through one of my dad's mates and tried to keep it a secret from the mechanics at the garage, in fear of certain jealousy and probable assault and battery. But four or five days before the final, Bill Shankly himself turned up at the garage to get his car washed. It was a metallic brown Ford Corsair with a vinyl roof, and no car has ever received more attention or more loving care in the 15 minutes it was there, as everyone who worked at the garage swarmed around it.

Shankly watched us with an amused smile, hands on hips, and then came the question they'd all been waiting for – 'Are you lads all right for tickets?' – which prompted a Shakespearean display of tragic misery. Shankly nodded in sympathy but said nothing, leaving us with a larger tip than normal. About an hour later, the Corsair returned to the forecourt, with Shankly leaning out of the window holding half a dozen ground tickets for Wembley. It was then that I had to confess I already had one, because I couldn't face committing an act of deceit on such a great man. Fortunately the mechanics were too overjoyed with Shankly's gift to extract punishment – their own 'jamminess' had now exceeded mine.

On the Thursday night I travelled on the overnight bus to London, arriving at Victoria coach station around seven o'clock the next morning. Apart from passing through on the school trip in 1966, and for the Cambridge interview in 1970, this was my first visit to London. Of course rather than brave the tube, I did the classic provincial number and tried to walk to Gloucester Road, getting lost on a dozen occasions, and feeling hopelessly inadequate and dwarfed by this thing called London. If anybody had stopped to tell me then that four years later I would be writing for *Time Out*, the inside guide to London, I'd have laughed all the way back to the coach station.

On the Friday night, all the ex-Prescotians met up in the student union of Imperial College for a session, which ended in mass singing of 'You'll Never Walk Alone', partly out of sheer exuberant drunkenness, partly as a retaliation to the 'Good Old Arsenal' dirge that appeared to be coming out of every radio in London, and which, to make matters worse, had been specially scripted by the man known only as 'The Chin', Jimmy Hill.

All you could hear on the tube up to Wembley the next morning was:

> *Good ol' Arsenal, We're proud to say that name*
> *And while we sing this song, We'll win the game!*

Although there was gradual resistance around the stadium itself with a typically witty Scouse reply, involving the same verse structure, but with lyrics embracing a proposal for Arsenal to go away and a prediction that they would win very little. Sadly that day, they won the Cup. Up in the steaming hot Liverpool terraces our gang were almost too wiped out to care as the match offered a totally enervating spectacle, as exhausted players, socks around their ankles, struggled to fill the spaces on the sun-baked pitch. Steve Heighway scored – well, he crossed and Arsenal's current goalkeeping coach Bob Wilson let the ball in – and then somebody in a yellow shirt – do we know to this day whether it was Eddie Kelly or George Graham? – toe-poked an equaliser past Ray Clemence, who was then so mesmerised by Charlie George's ugliness, that he lost the flight of a half-hit shot to concede the winner. Well, that's how it felt anyway.

The 18 or so in our group queued up for hours to get a train at Wembley Park, and then traipsed around London trying in vain to find a pub where 'Good Old Arsenal' wasn't being sung. The flawed logic of booking the return coach to Liverpool for the Sunday, in anticipation of a celebratory night on the town, now hit home, for there can be no worse place on earth than London when a local team has won the FA Cup. We ended up, God knows why, in the deserted bar of Guys Hospital, were we could drink and commiserate with one another. Until, that is, *Cup Final Match of the Day* came on, with The Chin hobnobbing with the Arsenal players at their banquet. It took about six of us to stop the school's six-foot-four-inch former hockey goalkeeper Colin Crabb from putting his size-14 boot through the television screen. We dispersed into the night, knowing that it was unlikely we'd go to a Liverpool match in such fraternity again. Going to Anfield had been part of the social glue throughout seven years of secondary school, and now we were all over the country, mingling with people who supported other teams or who didn't like football at all.

With the money accumulated from the various jobs I'd done since January – filing clerk, car-washer, Census officer, petrol-pump attendant – I went on a six-week hitch-hiking and ferry tour of Greece with two friends from school, Hedley Railton and Graham Birchenough, and another lad who had worked with me in the Planning Department, Paul Turnbull. We were all Liverpool fans, but spent more time on the holiday talking about music – Santana's *Abraxas* had just come out, not to mention Carole King's *Tapestry*, James Taylor's *Mud Slide Slim* and Marvin Gaye's *What's Going On?* – and these largely formed the soundtrack to the trip. We *did* manage one bizarre football fix – a friendly in Athens between

Olympiakos and . . . Stoke City. We were let in to the ground for nothing – presumably out of sympathy for appearing to support Stoke – while forty thousand Greeks filled the stadium, letting off flares and shouting guttural multisyllabic chants. We gradually discovered that the reason for the frenzy was that they all wanted to see Gordon Banks who, just a year earlier, had made that save from Pele's header in the Mexico World Cup.

But as the electronic scoreboard flashed up the teams, there was a rippling groan – John Farmer was in goal, and Banks wasn't even among the subs. A dismal match ended in a 2–1 win for Stoke, which resulted in the home fans, ourselves included for safety, spinning their polystyrene cushions up into the Athenian night in a gesture of disdain and then watching them flutter down to the pitch below, where they provided more spectacle than either Olympiakos or Stoke had managed.

The final Saturday of the trip was the first day of the new season. I managed to find the BBC World Service on the transistor I'd brought, which told me as I lay on a strip of Corfu beach that a lad barely older than myself had scored Liverpool's opening goal against Nottingham Forest. Kevin Keegan had arrived.

I didn't see him in action until our home game against Leicester City on 28 August. Keegan was everywhere, the original clockwork mouse, and the scorers in our 3–2 win reflected Liverpool's future for the next five years or so – Heighway, Keegan, Toshack. On Saturday, 25 September, I saw my last home game before leaving for university, a 2–2 draw against Manchester United, Bobby Graham and Brian Hall getting our goals, before United pulled back.

It could have all ended there. You could never call Cambridge 'the real world', but I knew that it would be a challenge to my old one. My parents had a fear that I would disown both them and my background once I started mingling with the sherry-drinking classes. But it didn't happen.

St Catharine's was one of their more egalitarian colleges of the time, and I found myself sharing space with Geordies, Mankies and Brummies, as well as the odd posh Chelsea supporter. My own playing career was even revived thanks to the purchase of a pair of

National Health glasses with plastic lenses and hooked arms. So being a Liverpool supporter wasn't, as I'd feared, a passport to the leper colony, just a cause for ribaldry from mates and amused puzzlement from the girls whose parties I disappeared from to watch *Match of the Day*.

My best friend at college turned out to be a Liverpool supporter too, an engineer called Ed Robinson – middle initial G, believe it or not – who, though he was from somewhere called Retford, had developed a passion for the Reds. It was a great pleasure to see his wonder-struck face when I took him for his first visit to the Kop during one of the vacations. We roomed together during our final year, watching and playing football – he won a much-cherished Blue – chasing girls from Homerton College and playing The Isley Brothers, Isaac Hayes and Brass Construction loudly out of the windows of our room.

We went to the 1974 Cup final together, dressed in red loons, and three years later we met up again to make the pilgrimage to Rome by train from Lime Street, five days of hell around one night of complete exultation. The next year he was one of seven who went to Wembley to watch us beat Bruges, and in 1981 Ed got married and as a wedding present I bought him and his new wife tickets for the European Cup final against Real Madrid in Paris, where he had cunningly arranged his honeymoon. My girlfriend of the time – a West Brom fanatic – also went to the game, even though we both knew we were splitting up. If we'd lost I'd really have felt bad . . .

Back in 1974, I'd applied for a job on the Liverpool *Daily Post*, secretly hoping that I might one day become the man who followed Liverpool's games for a living. But I didn't get the job, and went down to London to find work after seeing the Reds record their biggest-ever win – 11–0 – over Stromsgodset of Norway. I was truly an exile now, seeing the team more at away games than home. And it's been that way ever since.

The various Liverpool teams became one distant relative whom you were always pleased to see, whether they entertained you or otherwise, because each game you saw added to the 'family' memories, or brought news of a new arrival. It no longer hurt like it used to in my teens and twenties when they lost, and the disasters at Heysel and Hillsborough put any lingering passion to shame. Football isn't worth dying for.

When I see Liverpool now, it's mostly from the privileged view of the Anfield press box. Anyone's fear about the neutrality of my reporting can be safely dismissed – I am probably more critical of the home side than sycophantic, because the instinct remains to see them not only do well, but also to do it in style. One of the reasons the affection has lasted is that Liverpool have always produced teams who have kept a pleasing balance of priorities, between winning efficiently, playing it fair and allowing a substantial degree of self-expression.

Selecting a 'dream team' therefore made me feel like a manager who has to drop several players on the eve of a Cup final. Several choices were easy – Ray Clemence in goal, Tommy Smith and Alan Hansen in defence, Graeme Souness in midfield, and Dalglish and Rush in attack. I also chose John Barnes and Peter Thompson pretty swiftly, which left the two full-backs and a right-sided midfield player. Chris Lawler had been an early favourite so I stuck with him, while Alan Kennedy for it because he played with a smile, and scored some historic goals. Terry McDermott won the other midfield place because in his selfless running and his ability to score wonderful goals, he seemed to epitomise cherished Liverpool qualities. I chose Bob Paisley as a manager, partly because of his wonderful record of service to the club, and partly because I twice got to interview him, something I never achieved with the man who made it all happen, Bill Shankly.

POSTSCRIPT
Since I wrote this introduction five years ago, a great deal has changed at Liverpool Football Club. Gérard Houllier has come in as manager and stabilised what had become a listing vessel. Several players have come to prominence under him, most notably Michael Owen, Steven Gerrard and Sami Hyypiä, who are all surefire future 'Dream Team' members. But the Title, or Premiership, has yet to be won since 1990. That remains the real 'dream' of all Reds, whatever their generation.

Stan Hey
Wiltshire, 2002.

CHRIS LAWLER

The Silent Knight

If the chapter title reads like a strained pun, forgive me; but Chris Lawler's nickname at Anfield for a long time was 'Silent Night', because of his quiet demeanour. I amended this because, both as a young supporter and later as a more mature critic, I admired not only the way he played but also the grace and courtesy which Lawler brought to the game.

Although he is best known as an elegant right-back with a flair for scoring goals, Lawler began his football life, way back in the late 1950s, as a schoolboy centre-half. He played there for the England schools team, which he captained against West Germany at Wembley in front of a crowd of 90,000. Liverpool brought him in as a 15-year-old groundstaff boy in June 1959, six months before Bill Shankly arrived, and the next year he signed as a junior on his 16th birthday.

The groundstaff system may require some explanation to readers now accustomed to youth teams, football academies and schoolboy associations. It was designed to bring possible talent to a club before anybody else could snap them up, paying the lads a wage for services outside of football until they reached the age where proper contracts and professional training could begin. If it sounds fairly feudal, bear in mind that football 37 years ago was still clinging to a maximum wage of £20 a week for full-time professionals. When you think of the wealth that must have been generated by all those record post-war attendances, it begs the question of where the money went – certainly not on the players' wages, and not, for the most part, on the football grounds either.

Lawler remembers a typical week for a groundstaff boy, and also how one small moment changed the system at Liverpool: 'Basically the groundstaff were responsible for maintenance work – painting, decorating, plumbing and that sort of thing – and we worked five days a week from 8 a.m. to 5 p.m., and trained twice a week in the evenings with the amateur players. It was mostly for fitness, rather than football practice itself. One morning I was going off for a game of snooker during my tea-break – the club had a professional-sized table in among the offices – when Shankly stopped me and asked me where I was going. When I told I was playing snooker he threw a complete fit and gave me a mouthful. He couldn't believe the system allowed young players to behave like that. So the very next morning, he changed it all, and I was put in with the professionals. Liverpool had a big squad in those days, and people like Jimmy Melia, Alan A'Court and Bobby Campbell would always try and help and pass on advice. You basically learnt the game from the older players. A bit later on Joe Fagan came in as a coach and trainer, and he looked after me as well.'

In the autograph book that my dad's friend gave me, Chris Lawler's name features alongside the likes of Phil Ferns, Dick White, Johnny Morrisey, Ron Yeats, Bert Slater, John Molyneaux, Gerry Byrne and Ian St John, which confirms that he must have been among the 1961–62 professional squad. And he was soon playing in A-team games, one step down from the reserves, as a 16-year-old among professionals on the way down and older teenagers on the way up. He soon made progress into the reserves, coached by Fagan, who played their Central League games at Anfield, as preparation for the day when a player would turn out for the first time in front of a full house. Chris eventually made his first-team début, standing in for the injured Ron Yeats at centre-half, against West Brom at Anfield on 20 March 1963.

'Being picked for the first team didn't bother me, because I didn't know what to expect really, and I wasn't nervous about it. I didn't have a car at the time so I used to have to take two buses to get to the ground. When I got off at Arkles Lane, it was all very quiet, and not many people were around. It was only when I got to the ground itself that I realised the gates were already closed, and I began to get really nervous. I was all right once we started playing. I can't remember much about the game – a 2–2 draw – except that it was a relief when it was over.'

Lawler took part in five more league games that season, Liverpool's first back in the top division, playing not only at centre-half but also in both full-back positions. He stood in for the suspended Ron Yeats for three games in March, which embraced two in successive days over the Easter period – matches were played on Good Friday, Saturday and Easter Monday then, long before BSkyB arrived – and Liverpool won them all, conceding just one goal. Lawler also played in the FA Cup semi-final against Leicester City at Hillsborough, standing in for Jimmy Melia, but finished on the losing side as Liverpool went out to a single goal by Mike Stringfellow.

His friend and fellow ex-groundstaff lad, Tommy Smith, also made his début around that time, but the following season, 1963–64, when Liverpool won the Championship for the first time since 1947, Lawler played in only six games, again in the number 5 shirt, while Tommy didn't get called up once. It seemed that they would both have to wait for their chances, as Lawler recalls. 'Ron Yeats was firmly established as the centre-half, so I couldn't see a situation arising where I could get into the team on a regular basis. So I went to see Bill Shankly – Tommy went too, but separately – and we both put in transfer requests. Shanks was totally shocked, probably by our cheek as much as anything else, but he promised to have a think about it. And early the following season, he put me in at right-back when Gerry Byrne was switched to the left to replace Ronnie Moran.'

Lawler returned to the team for good on 26 September 1964 in the 5–1 home win over Aston Villa, and played in all the remaining 32 games of the season. On 5 December he scored the last goal in another 5–1 home win over Burnley and scored the winner in a 2–1 home win over Wolves in February 1965. Nobody quite knew then that those goals were a significant portent for Lawler's career to come, but the player himself had his own expectations. 'Even when I played at centre-half, I liked to get on the ball a bit – in fact I probably tried to play too much football for that position. It was just a natural instinct for me to go forward, and when I moved to right-back I had more freedom to do it because you could always be sure, if you gave them a shout, that someone in the team would cover for you.'

Liverpool consolidated, if that's the right word, in the league that year, finishing seventh, saving their energies for their two dramatic cup campaigns, at home and in Europe. In the FA Cup, they survived an early scare when they drew at home to Stockport County in the fourth round, but won the replay 2–0 away. Bolton and the much-hated Leicester City were beaten in the next rounds, before Chelsea fell in the semi-final.

Running concurrently with this campaign were the final stages of Liverpool's first adventure in the European Cup. Reykjavik and Anderlecht had been beaten in both legs in the autumn, but the German side Cologne proved tougher opposition, as they held Liverpool to two goalless draws, and then 2–2 in the replayed game in Rotterdam. Liverpool only went through on the toss of a coloured disc, as the concept of the penalty shoot-out was yet to be conceived. Those who deride penalties should ask themselves if tossing a piece of plastic after three hard-fought games in three different countries was a fitting way to decide a tie.

The Cologne replay was played on 24 March, followed by the FA Cup semi-final on 27 March. Liverpool won both: the FA Cup final against Leeds was played on 1 May, just three days before the first leg of the European Cup semi-final on 4 May. It was a tremendous climax to a season, as Lawler remembers: 'The crowd at Anfield and the fans who followed us away from home were incredible. But then it must have seemed like a dream after being stuck in the Second Division for eight seasons. And the European games were really exciting because it was a totally new experience for all of us. If anything, they suited me more, because I got more chances to attack, and often spent more of my time in the opposition half than in ours. The FA Cup final was a great occasion, because of the fans, and because we won, but I'm afraid it's true what most players say about it, because it did pass by very quickly. It's almost impossible to appreciate it at the time. It only really hit me when I actually went up to collect my medal. I think I had a fairly quiet game, because the lad I was marking, Leeds United's South African winger Albert Johansen, completely froze on that day. I was pretty nervous too, to tell the truth.'

Chris couldn't remember it, but he actually played a vital part in Liverpool's first goal, scored by Roger Hunt in the first half of extra-time. Next time he watches it on video, he'll see that Leeds look set to break up a Liverpool attack on the right, and have cleared the ball forward only for him to launch into an overhead kick to intercept. The ball is then headed down by Roger Hunt to Willie Stevenson, who immediately tracks left into space across the pitch and, as Gerry Byrne goes on an overlap, Stevenson threads a pass into the box, Byrne crosses and Hunt heads home. In the modern, fantasy-league terminology, Lawler's contribution would certainly count as an assist.

Lawler's momentous weekend wasn't completed by being part of the first Liverpool team to win the FA Cup in 72 years of trying, nor by the return to the city and the parade on the Sunday. For, on the Monday, he had arranged to be married, not expecting the ceremony to be squeezed between an FA Cup final and a European Cup semi-final.

'We'd already booked it for that day, thinking the season would be over by then. But it wasn't. So I trained in the morning, which was the day before the Inter Milan game, and then I went and got married. We had a reception and everything, cut the cake, made all the speeches, but then I had to report to the team's hotel, and ended up spending the night in the same room as Tommy Smith. He had his bed pushed up against the wall and said, "You're not coming anywhere near me!"'

Like anyone who was there that night, Chris considers the atmosphere at Anfield which he experienced in the Inter Milan game to be 'the best ever'. It helped that Liverpool had won the Cup and that they played such rampant football on an occasion when they might have looked at the opposition – the reigning European and World Champions – and wilted. For Lawler, though, there might have been even greater glory, as he was the scorer of a great goal that was cruelly disallowed, and which would have almost certainly won the tie.

'I got the ball from a throw-in, and just took it on a bit, and before I knew what was happening I'd gone past a couple of their lads and was on the edge of the area, so I just whacked the ball and it went straight into the far top corner. But the flag had gone up because Geoff Strong had strayed offside. These days they'd probably allow the goal, because Geoff wasn't interfering with play – so who knows what would have happened if it had gone in?'

Still, Liverpool's 3–1 lead on the night looked impressive enough, but a team which had played only four previous away games in Europe were always likely to be vulnerable to their first exposure to the fevered atmosphere of San Siro stadium in Milan, which held 90,000 fans that night.

Although some of the refereeing decisions for the second leg were genuinely atrocious, Lawler thinks that the hostile environment helped get Milan the 3-0 result they needed: 'Bill Shankly told us to go out and have a look at the pitch when we arrived at the stadium, and it was probably the worst thing we could have done. There were rockets being fired from the crowd, and all these red flares being lit. It was actually quite frightening, and I think all that put us off a bit. I mean, one of these rockets dropped out of the sky and just missed my head.'

The disappointment of that night was augmented by defeat in the European Cup-Winners' Cup final against Borussia Dortmund the next year. It couldn't yet be translated into the vital experience for future campaigns but, as Chris suggests, 'You can bet that the boys in the boot-room made notes about everything they saw, and that definitely helped all the other Liverpool teams in Europe later on.'

One of the items in the boot-room log-book after the 1966 European campaign might well have been Lawler's dramatic ability to drift forward and get goals. He scored four of Liverpool's 11 *en route* to the final, one in the 2–1 home victory against Juventus, two in the 3–1 home win over Standard Liège, and another in the 2–0 win against Honved. Lawler's particular style was to drift slowly upfield during open play or, more often, to arrive late into the penalty area for a set-piece corner or free-kick. It was all done by stealth, not by the brute force of slinging a big centre-half upfield to see if he could get on the end of something.

'Chris was the footballer in our defence, just like Alan Hansen was later,' says Tommy Smith, Lawler's room-mate, friend and defensive partner through over ten seasons. 'For a big lad, he had a good touch on the ball, and he was impressive in the air. He wasn't the greatest tackler, though, but he made up for that with his goals at the other end.'

In Liverpool's second Championship season under Shankly, Lawler notched five goals in 40 games, to add to the four he scored in Europe, and he became the epitome of the modern, attacking full-back. Ray Clemence, who arrived at Liverpool in 1967, and who went on to enjoy several seasons with Chris as his right-back, gives this perspective on his play: 'The number of goals he scored in free play, never mind the set-piece situations, was astonishing. None of them were penalties either. He used to sneak into positions like Martin Peters, only Chris was a full-back. He wasn't particularly quick but his reading of the game was superb whether in defence or attack. If you can imagine him being around now with the wing-back system, he'd walk into the England team. He was doing then what Gary Neville is doing now, *and* getting goals.'

In the 1966–67 season, however, Liverpool ran into a football force that was probably several years in advance of them. A first-round European Cup tie brought them up against the relatively unknown Ajax Amsterdam who, rather like Liverpool, had embraced new tactics and playing systems under their influential coach Rinus Michels, as the game became both faster and more technical. Even so, Ajax barely had five or six full-time professionals in their side when they played the first leg against Liverpool. Unfortunately for the Reds, one of them happened to be the 19-year-old prodigy Johan Cruyff.

On 7 December, in fog so dense that Bill Shankly was able to wander onto the pitch on several occasions without the referee seeing him, Liverpool suffered what remains their worst defeat in

Europe, losing 5–1, their consolation goal coming in the last minute from Chris Lawler.

'The game should never have been played,' Lawler says, not out of bitterness at the result, but because the conditions were so bizarre and plainly unsettling to Liverpool. But that was no excuse for the defeat. 'We totally underestimated them,' he says, 'and nobody had told us about Cruyff. That sort of thing wouldn't happen later on.'

Shankly had indeed dismissed the threat of Ajax out of hand. In an interview with a Dutch journalist before the first leg, and published in Anfield's programme for the second, Shankly had accused 'most continental teams of doing a lot of bluffing', even fingering the brilliant Hungarian team that had beaten England 6–3 at Wembley in 1953! Such blind chauvinism might have had its place in wartime to fire up the troops, but it wouldn't work in the increasingly sophisticated world of European football. In any case, Ajax proved their football had been no fluke by drawing 2–2 at Anfield in the return, with Cruyff scoring both goals. It was Jock Stein, manager of Celtic, rather than Bill Shankly, who had the answers in Europe that year.

Liverpool's simple approach to football was all very commendable but, as Lawler recalls, team practices and meetings were also kept to a minimum: 'It was all pretty basic, five-a-side games with a bit more detail thrown in occasionally. We never practised corners or free-kicks – the idea was just to play football off the cuff. And we never talked about the opposition much. Maybe because there was quite a lot of tough competition in those days, there were certainly more teams on an equal level than there are now.'

Manchester United, their City neighbours, Leeds, Everton and then Arsenal all won the league after Liverpool's 1966 triumph, emphasising the spread of power as opposed to the concentration of it which we have today.

Liverpool continued to play well, without quite doing enough to bring another trophy to Anfield. 'There was a good spirit in that 1960s team, Lawler remembers fondly. 'We were all on the same basic wage, £45 a week, the same bonuses and there were no arguments in the dressing-room.'

But Liverpool's first great side, though we didn't quite know it yet, had already peaked, although Lawler and Tommy Smith as younger team members would play through as the rebuilding began to take place after the disastrous FA Cup defeat at Watford in February 1970. Lawler played in that game and remembers the immediate consequences: 'On the Monday morning, we all reported for training as usual, knowing that Shanks had not been very happy about the performance and he came out and picked a team for a practice game which included Ray Clemence in goal, Larry Lloyd in defence and Alun Evans in the number 9 shirt, and everybody knew it was all over for the likes of Tommy Lawrence, Ron Yeats, Ian St John and Roger Hunt.'

In fact Shankly resorted to using 23 players in the first team that season, when his preferred number would have been 12 fewer. Lawler, though, was a model of consistency, playing in all 42 league games, and scoring ten goals, just three fewer than the side's most successful striker Bobby Graham. With Tommy Smith assuming the captaincy, Lawler also took on a pastoral role as one of the few senior pros left in the side.

'I'd take it on myself to talk to the younger lads in the squad, trying to help them out the way the older pros had once helped me when I was a kid. It wasn't anything serious, just stuff about how to conduct yourself, on and off the field. We had a tour to Sweden during one pre-season, and that helped everyone get to know one another better as characters and start pulling together.'

The new Liverpool team gelled to such an extent that they reached the 1971 FA Cup final against Arsenal, after beating Southampton, Spurs and Everton in the later rounds. Everton had also been beaten earlier in the season in a dramatic derby at Anfield, when Liverpool came back from 2–0 down, with Chris Lawler getting into the penalty area to fire the winner in front of an ecstatic Kop, after Steve Heighway and John Toshack had brought us back into the game.

There was much optimism then, but playing an Arsenal side which was packed with experienced players who had just won the Championship proved too much for Liverpool at Wembley, as

Lawler recalls. 'It was a boiling hot day and we had these shirts which weighed a ton, while Arsenal had these lightweight Aertex numbers. We were just too inexperienced as a team. That game was the only time I ever got cramp in the whole of my career.'

Shankly's changes finally brought the desired results in the 1972–73 season, when an improving young team, built around Emlyn Hughes, Kevin Keegan, John Toshack and Smith and Lawler, swept to the Championship and the UEFA Cup. Lawler was again an ever-present in the league, and also played in all the UEFA Cup games, bringing all his previous experience to bear. As Tommy Smith lifted the cup in Germany after holding out against Borussia Moenchengladbach, only he and Lawler remained from the Liverpool side which had first won the FA Cup back in 1965, and now here they were in the first Liverpool team to win a European trophy. Both genuine Scousers too!

Lawler began what was to be pretty much his final season, reining back his attacking instincts. 'I'd got the blame for a goal we'd conceded after I'd gone forward, so I decided that I'd start to stay put, do my own job and just mark my winger. Then we had a home game against Tottenham and everyone was telling me to go forward for corners but I just ignored them. Finally I went up for one, and immediately scored, and then stayed back again until the last minute of the game when I went up and headed the winner. I never got any stick after that.'

But a cartilage injury soon cut Lawler down that season, and although he made it back to be substitute at the 1974 FA Cup final, in which Liverpool beat Newcastle 3–0, he knew that his Anfield days were numbered, as his old mate Tommy Smith began to make the right-back spot his own.

'It's a gradual thing, but you can see it coming, and so you have to move on,' he says. 'It's hard being a footballer when it gets to that stage. I'd learned early on that there was no sentiment in football by seeing how footballers I'd admired were treated when they finished. At least I got a testimonial game, several years after I'd left, but it was a difficult time for me. My daughter died, and I don't think I made the right decision to go to Portsmouth, because of all the travel. I still felt part of Liverpool, part of the family.'

Lawler played and coached all over the world in the ensuing years – America, Stockport, Bangor City, Norway – before Joe Fagan invited him back to the club as reserve-team coach. Two Central League titles followed, but when Kenny Dalglish took over as manager, Lawler's quiet style proved not to his liking, and he was asked to leave.

'Kenny wanted his own way, which is fair enough, but it was just the way it was handled that upset me at the time. Now I go back to the club and there are no problems. I still see Roy Evans, Ronnie Moran and Tom Saunders for a cup of tea and a chat, although I never discuss the team with them – they've got enough on their plates as it is. I don't miss playing at all. There was too much tension. The only time you could enjoy it was when you were winning easily with about a minute to go.'

Chris now lives on Anglesey in a beautiful spot overlooking a windswept bay. His hair has greyed since the 1960s but there's still a shine in his eyes and a chuckle in his voice when he talks about the old Liverpool. These days, he helps coach Porthmadog in the Welsh League – 'They're good lads, but we can only pay them about £35 a week, which is what I was getting 30-odd years ago. Some things never change, because we didn't get the big money in them days either.'

TOMMY SMITH

Anfield's Iron and Soul

'Tommy Smith wasn't born – he was quarried,' David Coleman once said in a commentary on *Match of the Day* in the early 1970s, as Liverpool's young captain ploughed successfully through another ball-winning tackle. Although obviously from the *Blue Peter* school of 'one I prepared earlier', the line was good enough to be remembered and repeated but it shouldn't be allowed to rest as a summation of Tommy's career. Yes, he was a hard man at a time when tackling was less policed than it is now, but he was also a player of considerable skill and of unquenchable spirit. And he was, and is, funny with it.

Peter Thompson tells a story of an early training session at Melwood after he had joined from Preston in August 1963. Determined to impress his new colleagues with his skill, Thompson neatly nutmegged the team's giant centre-half and captain Ron Yeats, only to find himself grabbed by the shirt-front. 'Do that again and I'll break your bloody leg, son!' Yeats thundered, quickly being joined by the defence's other hard man Gerry Byrne, who offered Thompson a similar warning. And then, from nowhere, up stepped Tommy Smith to assert that he would exact the same punishment if the trick was ever tried on him.

'He was only about 18 years old and still a reserve,' Thompson recalls with a smile, 'and here he was laying down the law. You had to admire his cheek.'

Tommy Smith joined Liverpool in 1960 as a 15-year-old member of the groundstaff straight from a schoolboy playing career which included representing the city in the FA's national schools competition. His father had died a year earlier, and his widowed mother took him down to Anfield to meet Bill Shankly. 'He was a great man,' Tommy recalled as we talked at Melwood some 37 years after his first arrival. 'He offered me £7 a week, which was a lot of money in those days when the playing wage was only about £20 a week – that's all they could earn. I'll always be grateful to him. He shaped my life to a certain degree with a famous old saying – "Don't take any shit from anybody, son, and as long as you play it straight, there'll be no problem" – and that's what I've tried to do over the years. I know I've had some sort of reputation as being a hard man, but that was only when there was a ball there!'

Tommy became a full-time professional on his 17th birthday in April 1962, and his progress at the club was already being made known to the fans who only watched the first team in action. Indeed it was probably highly appropriate that, on the night that Liverpool were presented with the Second Division Championship trophy after the game against Charlton Athletic on Monday, 30 April, the match programme featured him in its series of 'Anfield Personalities'. You can almost hear a clipped Movietone voice describing him:

A *powerfully* built lad for his age – he is just over five foot nine inches, and close on 12 stone – he is showing considerable promise, being extremely good with his head and able to use either foot with almost equal skill. After progressing through the junior teams he was given his chance in the Central League team last season, making five appearances and proving his adaptability by occupying both defensive and attacking positions. The same versatility has been apparent again this season, during which he has been a regular in the Central League XI. He has figured at right- and left-half, inside-left and centre-forward and has played so well in all these positions that it is still difficult to say which will eventually prove his best. He is steadily gaining in experience and, like so many of his young colleagues on the staff, looks to have all the attributes necessary to make the top grade in due course.

It was during his reserve-team phase that I first saw Tommy,

39

watching with my dad who always liked to consider himself a talent scout. I can remember Dad saying something about Tommy's thigh muscles looking like a pair of giant hams, but having not long seen *The Lost World* I had this image of him being built like a dinosaur, probably a Tyrannosaurus Rex, for that was certainly how he used to rampage through the opposing stiffs. At the same time it was noticeable that he had small, almost delicate feet for his size, with a lovely touch on the ball. His distribution (as they call it now) or passing (as we called it then) was also a feature, while in that 1961–62 reserve season he'd also notched seven goals – not bad for a primarily defensive player.

Shankly's rapid rebuilding of the team in the early 1960s had included the recruitment of fellow Scots Ron Yeats from Dundee United and Ian St John from Motherwell, the latter forming an instant alliance with Roger Hunt, who scored 41 goals, a club record, in that promotion season. Shankly, apparently, had been under no illusions about the task of reviving both the team and the ground. 'This is the biggest shithouse in the world, this place,' he once told the young Tommy Smith. But he also knew that refurbishing the stadium would have to wait until the team established itself in the top division. With the Reds finishing in eighth place, and reaching an FA Cup semi-final, their first season back was good enough for most fans, and for Tommy Smith the tail-end of the season, the last home game in fact, offered a major highlight – his first-team début.

He wore the number 4 shirt in a 5–1 Wednesday evening thrashing of Birmingham City – pub quiz devotees and John Motson please note that a T. Smith (Trevor) also played for the Blues that night – with Hunt getting two of the goals.

Tommy remembers the game probably more vividly than many of the great occasions in the rest of his career: 'I'd just had my 18th birthday in April and making my début against Birmingham, as a Liverpool lad and a Liverpool supporter, made me feel something I'd never felt in my life before – it was like going to the moon. I felt 20 feet tall. I came out of the ground afterwards and my mum and step-father said, "Come on, let's get home and have a cup of tea," but I wanted to bask in the glory for a bit longer. I just walked around the streets for a couple of hours and when I got home, honest, I could have died that night and been quite happy.'

During the 1963 close season, Shankly, ever restless for improvement, strengthened the Liverpool squad by signing Peter Thompson from Preston North End for £35,000, while the elegant Scottish wing-half Willie Stevenson had established himself in the team over the last 28 games of the 1962–63 season. Tommy Lawrence had taken over from Jim Furnell in goal, while some of the stalwarts from the Second Division days – Tommy Leishman, Kevin Lewis and Alan A'Court – were being eased out. There was a future for the younger players like Tommy Smith, but not just yet, with the result that he spent the entire Championship season of 1963–64 gaining further experience in the reserves. But the challenge of the European Cup in 1964–65, and an early-season injury to Ian St John began to open doors for Tommy.

He wore St John's number 9 shirt for four games, and acquitted himself well, scoring one goal against Blackburn Rovers and another against Leeds United. But it was on 25 November 1964 that Smith made his greatest impact so far, being brought into the home leg of the second-round European Cup-tie against the Belgian champions, RSC Anderlecht.

Liverpool had dismissed Reykjavik by an aggregate score of 11–1 in the first round – the Kop teased their own team by booing them in the second half and cheering every Reykjavik touch – but the Anderlecht tie was a serious business. The Belgian national team, most of which was selected from the Anderlecht club, had recently drawn 2–2 against England at Wembley.

Shankly duly pulled two master-strokes of kidology. First he fired up his team beforehand by telling them that the Belgians were rubbish, and then he played Tommy Smith in the number 10 shirt which, the programme had suggested, was supposed to be worn by a forward, Bobby Graham. In fact Smith was deployed as a free-floating defender, which completely flummoxed the Anderlecht players.

Smith recalls the night with a laugh: 'It certainly confused them, especially their wing-half who began chasing me back into our defence. It was just that in those days everything was new. It was a 4-4-2 system which a lot of people think England started, but I can honestly say that it was Liverpool who were one of the first teams to actually play that way. I came across it playing for the England Youth Team in Switzerland – they used to call it the 'Swiss Bolt'. The boss brought it in for us, and we perfected it. We used to hold the line and let people run offside, we never actually moved up to catch them. It was a nice way of playing because it was interesting, and it put an awful lot of emphasis on us keeping it tight at the back, and the forwards scoring goals, which we did in those days. It gave us a freedom to play, but basically we had a great side at that time too.'

Liverpool scored three goals inside 50 minutes against Anderlecht that night – from St John, Hunt and Yeats – and ran out easy winners. Afterwards Shankly revealed his true feelings about the Belgians by congratulating his players 'for beating one of the best teams in the world'. Liverpool won the away leg too, with a single goal from Roger Hunt.

For Tommy Smith the tie had been a wonderful endorsement of his abilities as a marker and ball-playing defender in the most testing of circumstances – facing experienced foreign internationals whose tricks and moves would have been completely unfamiliar to an 18-year-old with only five first-team games to his credit.

Smith was quickly brought into the side who played at Burnley on 5 December, winning 5–1, and was then a fixture in Liverpool teams for the next 13 seasons.

Being part of the first Liverpool side to win the FA Cup and reaching the semi-final of the European Cup were certainly achievements Smith is proud of, though he is typically combative, even after all these years, about the way Inter Milan won 3–0 at home in 1965, with two controversial goals, to go through to the final: 'We got robbed by a referee who got paid. He got done later, but that was too late for us. We'd have beaten Benfica in the final, no question about it, and then we'd have been the first British side to have won it, before Celtic or Manchester United.'

But the following season brought swift compensation. Shankly had created a side so finely balanced that he barely needed to change it – only 14 players were used throughout the whole Championship season, and of those Bobby Graham played in just one game. In our classroom Lawrence, Lawler, Byrne, Smith, Yeats, Stevenson, Milne, Callaghan, Hunt, St John, Thompson was recited more often than anything our Latin or French teachers could come up with.

The highlight of the year was the 5–0 win over Everton at Anfield on 25 September 1965, sparked by Tommy Smith's diving header in the first half. Roger Hunt scored two, St John one and Willie Stevenson produced a wonderful chip on the run to beat Gordon 'Girlie' West in the Everton goal. And just to prove that the previous year in Europe had been no fluke, Liverpool went all the way to the 1966 Cup-Winners' Cup final, having beaten Juventus, Standard Liège, Honved and Celtic on the way. Celtic had beaten us 1–0 at Parkhead, and held out for an hour at Anfield before Tommy Smith battered home a low free-kick and six minutes later the injured Geoff Strong managed to stretch for the winning header. The Celtic fans' attempts to initiate a bottle-bank on the pitch was a minor diversion in an epic victory. My dad had been right to ban me from going – it was a man's night, and Tommy Smith was in his element.

Liverpool lost the final against Borussia Dortmund in extra-time when Libuda's long-range lob hit a post and bounced in off Ron Yeats as he ran back to clear. But that summer, as 'Sir' Roger Hunt, Ian Callaghan and Gerry Byrne helped the England squad become World Champions, it seemed inevitable that Liverpool would conquer Europe soon, while still dominating the domestic scene. Tommy Smith certainly felt confident enough: 'We had a system in those days where we could close the ball down; if the opposition got the ball we closed them down, we won the ball, and spread it out and played a bit of football. And the players we had – the likes of Ian Callaghan and Peter Thompson – could outrun anybody. These people could run – and Ian St John wasn't exactly slow, Roger was a great goalscorer. It was Shankly's initiative to get all these players together, a little bit of youth and a lot of experience, and we had a great side.'

But some evidence of frailty soon arrived in the 1966–67 season. We needed a replay in Brussels to see off a provincial Romanian side lyrically entitled Petrolul Ploesti – the Kop baited them with the 'Esso Sign Means Happy Motoring' song during the Anfield leg. And then, early in December, Liverpool ran into a new force in European football, Ajax Amsterdam.

Typically, Shankly wouldn't accept that Ajax were any good, or that the tie was over. By the time the second leg took place on 14 December Shankly had stoked up a fervour of expectation. Even the normally modest programme notes sounded a baroque warning to the visitors: 'with the fervent Anfield crowd to spur our team on in their usual enthusiastic fashion, we are not without hope by a long chalk'.

It was truly terrifying on the Kop that night, for the supporters rather than Ajax. Liverpool attacked with a demonic frenzy, with the result that the Kop was in almost constant movement. With steam rising from the closely packed bodies – and other natural elements – it was really hard to breathe and soon those who had fainted from the crush were being passed down to the pitch over the heads of the heaving mass. All I can remember now is the clammy fear, and the two goals each which Hunt and Cruyff scored. Oh, and the fact that Liverpool played in a bizarre strip of yellow shirts and black shorts which was abandoned immediately afterwards because of its link with a bad night in the team's history. (Yet another milestone to which we beat Manchester United.)

The team's sudden vulnerability may have something to do with the three previous seasons of heady success finally exacting a toll on tired bodies. But Smithy certainly wasn't one of them. He was an ever-present throughout this nightmare season in which Everton knocked us out of the Cup and United won the League. From having had things our own way for a while, suddenly we were faced with success for these unspeakable enemies, while the likes of Leeds United, Nottingham Forest and Spurs were thoroughly competitive teams. Even Fulham held us to a 2–2 draw at home – they did have Bobby Robson and Johnny Haynes still playing for them – in a game in which I witnessed the beginning of a long-standing 'friendship' between Tommy Smith and striker Allan Clarke. Clarke scored both Fulham's goals that day, 8 October 1966, one of which involved an audacious dribble along the by-line, past Smithy and other defenders, before he flicked the ball nonchalantly past Tommy Lawrence. Clarke celebrated the goal in vainglorious and provocative fashion, announcing himself to the crowd, and to Tommy, as a big-head. This and the five-a-side, piss-taking element of the goal had our number 4 steaming. He ploughed into the back of Clarke; Clarke back-heeled Tommy; they had words; they kicked lumps out of one another. This one ran and ran, especially after Clarke signed for Don Revie's beloved Leeds United.

In 1978, when I first interviewed Tommy Smith for *Time Out's* preview of Liverpool's second European Cup final, it became clear that Clarke ranked only marginally higher in Tommy Smith's demonology than his own club captain and team-mate Emlyn Hughes. The common factor these two characters shared was an all-too-obvious self-admiration, but Clarke's particular crime was, allegedly, that he liked 'doing' defenders when they, and the referee, weren't looking. And Tommy didn't like that at all.

To some non-Liverpudlian ears, this may sound like a case of the 'biter bit', but being as dispassionate as I can, I think Tommy Smith operated under a genuine code of ethics as far as his hard-man activities were concerned. The physical challenge, or 'putting a foot in' as he prefers to call it, was an essential feature of the game in the 1960s and '70s for both defenders and forwards alike. There was a whole generation of front men – the likes of Derek Dougan of Leicester City and Wolves, Wyn Davies of Newcastle United, Martin Chivers of Spurs, Mike Summerbee of Manchester City, Andy Lochhead of Burnley, Bobby Gould of Coventry City, Peter Osgood of Chelsea – who all knew how to look after themselves. Two forwards of that era, Johnny Morrisey of Everton and Bertie Auld of Celtic, even made it into Jack Charlton's 'little black book' for the, er, 'trouble' they caused him. Tackling hard but fairly was an acceptable practice on either side of the cultural divide between defenders and forwards; doing it on the sly was not, and I think Tommy Smith embodied that distinction.

Liverpool's signing of Tony Hateley, father of Mark, from Chelsea in the summer of 1967, was a tacit acknowledgement of the need for more physical power up front, particularly in the air, which was Hateley's speciality. Indeed, in one game in September that year, he scored a goal against his old club with a diving header when the ball was no more than nine inches off the turf. If he'd had a left foot it would have been a million times easier to score, but Tony chose to head the ball. It was no surprise then that he was cruelly nicknamed 'Douglas Bader' by many Kopites – good in the air, useless on the ground. It was strongly rumoured that Tommy Smith 'sorted out' Hateley at the club's training ground one morning after a disagreement, and he was soon on his way out of Anfield.

The teenager Alun Evans was signed for an astonishing £100,000 from Wolves in an attempt to boost Liverpool's scoring power, but third place in the 1968 Championship was followed by a frustrating second place to Leeds in 1969. The defence was playing really well – it conceded only 24 goals in 42 games in the 1968–69 season when Tommy Smith was an ever-present – but Liverpool won less than half of their home games the following season, and consequently finished fifth to Everton.

More painfully, Liverpool were embarrassingly knocked out of the FA Cup in the sixth round by Watford, Barry Endean's header past a flapping Tommy Lawrence sounding the death-knell for a generation of players upon whom Shankly had relied for seven or eight seasons. Tommy Smith was fortunate not to be playing that February day in 1970, but he was soon made aware of the implications of the defeat.

'Shanks wasn't too happy with the performance that day to say the least.' recalls Tommy. 'He seemed to realise that some of the players were getting on a bit, and more or less overnight he decided to split up the team. He asked me to take over as captain and I was told to keep it tight at the back and not lose goals for a few seasons while he tried to bring a new team into being, which he did very well. We managed to get to the FA Cup final in 1971 – losing to Arsenal – but we weren't really a great side yet, frankly, and there was still a lot of work to be done. But suddenly we started to take off again in the 1972–73 season, as Kevin Keegan, John Toshack and Stevie Heighway started to blossom.'

During these three and a half seasons of reconstruction, I happen to think that Tommy Smith's captaincy was little short of heroic. Liverpool's success in the 1960s had been based on a largely unchanging team and an unchanging pattern of play. Now there were up to a dozen new players trying to establish themselves as the hard core of the old team – Lawrence, Yeats, Hunt, St John, Byrne, Peter Thompson – were pensioned off. There was bound to be a high failure rate. Alun Evans soon faded, probably a legacy of being 'bottled' in the face in a night-club fight; Jack Whitham came from Sheffield Wednesday, scored a hat-trick at home against Derby County in December 1971, but never really clicked; John McLaughlin, Phil Boersma and Roy Evans were promoted from the reserves but couldn't establish themselves; while Alec Lindsay, who had been signed from Bury, looked a complete tortoise at left-half until he was switched to left-back where he had time to see the hares coming.

Against that, Ray Clemence, Larry Lloyd, John Toshack and most of all Kevin Keegan began to gel with the remaining core of the team – Emlyn Hughes, Chris Lawler, Ian Callaghan and captain Tommy Smith. In the 1971–72 season Liverpool finished third, just a point behind the new Champions Derby County, with my personal highlight being the 3–0 win against United at Old Trafford at Easter, a game I watched with discreet glee from the Stretford End with my Mancunian college pal, Richard White, who kindly refrained from pointing out to the United fans a Scouser in their midst.

A settled team, as in the '60s, was beginning to emerge: Clemence, Lawler, Lindsay, Smith, Lloyd, Hughes, Keegan, Hall, Heighway, Toshack, Callaghan, with Tommy as its physical and spiritual leader. Ray Clemence, who was brought into the team immediately after the Watford débâcle, recalls the influence Tommy Smith exerted as captain: 'He was a great leader on and off the field. The stories about Tommy's hardness are legendary, and they were quite deserved as well. If he saw anybody in trouble on the field he'd make sure that he got them out of it. And he was the same if we went out anywhere in the evening – if he could see a problem arising, he'd come and sort it out, not necessarily in a physical way, but just to stop the problem getting out of hand. He was always a player and person who, if you were straight with him, he'd be straight with you. But if he felt you'd try to cross him anywhere, you had a problem.

'Fortunately, I always got on well with him, and we're still great friends. I owe him a lot, and appreciate what he did for me as a goalkeeper. He was a hard man to work behind – he demanded things of you. When I first came into the side, he made sure that I knew what was required of a Liverpool keeper: that, as young as I was, I had to take responsibility in certain situations in terms of controlling the area and coming out for crosses.

'He was very unfortunate, Tommy, that he was in an era when Bobby Moore dominated that position, because he would have won a lot more England caps. He was a superb defender and he could also use the ball as well.'

In the 1972–73 season, Tommy Smith captained Liverpool to their first ever 'double', with a small 'd', when they won both the League and the UEFA Cup, their first trophies in seven seasons. The team's home form was superb, losing only one game – 0–2 to Arsenal in February – and dropping only five points out of a maximum 42. Peter Cormack, a wonderfully delicate Scottish midfield player signed from Nottingham Forest, proved to be a great provider for Keegan and Toshack, who scored 13 goals apiece. Indeed every first-choice outfield player Liverpool used that season registered at least a couple of goals. The title was won in style with a 2–0 home victory over Leeds United on Easter Monday, with Cormack and Keegan getting the goals in front of a packed 55,738 crowd.

In the UEFA Cup, Liverpool's triumph involved beating four German teams, two from the East, two from the West. Eintracht Frankfurt were seen off 2–0 on aggregate in the first round, Dynamo Berlin 3–1 in the third round, and Dynamo Dresden were beaten both home and away for a 3–0 aggregate. Liverpool were then a little lucky to squeeze past Spurs in the semi-final on the away-goals rule, and the first leg of the final against Borussia

Moenchengladbach was a real drama.

The home leg was initially abandoned after about half an hour because of a torrential rainstorm, but in the short time that football was played Shankly and his boot-room team had perceived an aerial weakness in the German defence. John Toshack, not selected for the original game, was quickly pressed into service and his headers helped set up two goals for Keegan, while Larry Lloyd headed the third from a corner. Ray Clemence also contributed a penalty save, which proved vital in the context of Borussia's 2–0 win in their home leg. But Liverpool had their first European trophy, and Tommy Smith's biggest problem was lifting it – 'The bloody thing felt as though it weighed three tons, and I was absolutely knackered, but I managed to get it into the air!'

During that season, however, when Smith had missed a few games, his understudy Phil Thompson had performed brilliantly at centre-half, creating the kind of selection problem that managers are said to enjoy, having two good players competing for one position. In the 1973–74 season Smith and Thompson swapped the number 4 shirt several times until the younger Scouser began to assert himself. Indeed, Smith discovered to his dismay that Shankly had been talking to Stoke City about a loan deal for him but it fell through and the player stayed put, albeit with a more dispassionate view of the club.

'When Shanks tried to sell me to Stoke my attitude did change. From being a one-club man I decided that I was ready to go anywhere so long as I could play football. I suppose that from then I began to see it as just a job, and not a duty.'

But anyone thinking of writing off Smithy was mistaken. By December he'd forced himself back into the team, having taken over from his fellow 1960 recruit, Chris Lawler, at right-back. When Larry Lloyd moved on later in the season to Coventry City, Emlyn Hughes switched to central defence alongside Thompson, with Smith and Lindsay as the full-backs, and Liverpool had one of the best football-playing back-fours in the league, a style that was impressively built on by Bob Paisley and his successors, Joe Fagan and Kenny Dalglish.

'We started playing more in a "sweeper" formation,' Smith recalls, 'but the overall style didn't change that much. We played it wide and kept possession, which were always two of our basic aims. It never varied to the extent that it was major surgery.'

The season was a patchy one, perhaps as a reaction to the previous year's success. Any hopes we had of capturing the European Cup were destroyed by two defeats at the highly talented feet of Red Star Belgrade, who won both second-round legs 2–1. The victory at Anfield was traumatic but ultimately educational, as the Miljan Miljanic-coached Yugoslavs simply passed the ball around all night in moving triangles and scored with two spectacular shots past Clemence. If that game was a fair measure of how far Liverpool still had to travel before they could reach the European summit, it also offered the club a route map on how to achieve it.

To add to this disappointment, the team's league form fell away in the last two months of the season, as they won only one of their last eight games, thereby gifting the title to Leeds. But the excitement of winning through to another Cup final may have had some effect.

I distinctly remember the first goalless semi-final against Leicester at Old Trafford on Saturday, 30 March, during which Tommy Smith celebrated Red Rum's first Grand National victory as it was flashed onto the information screen at the Scoreboard End. Presumably he'd had a tip from Southport trainer Ginger McCain – or maybe it was a chance bet? – but it suggested that the team's collective mind wasn't entirely on the job. In the replay at Villa Park it was, and Leicester were emphatically beaten 3–1, Keegan scoring one of his best goals for us, a wonderful lob volley on the run.

The final itself was hopelessly one-sided as Newcastle United eventually folded under Liverpool's attacking pressure in the second half. Tommy Smith remembers another reason for the team's assertive performance – 'Malcolm Macdonald had been shouting his mouth off in the papers all week before the game, and all that got passed around the dressing-room, so though we didn't need motivating, that did the trick.'

Keegan and Heighway got the first two goals – my seat at

Wembley was dead level with the Newcastle area, which made up for the lousy view I'd had in 1971 – and Tommy Smith played a key part in the extended passing move which allowed Keegan to tap in for the third. If you watch that build-up again on video – it's unlikely to be on sale in the Newcastle area – Tommy Smith's skill and movement off the ball from his nominal position at right-back are almost arrogant in their accomplishment.

Keegan is on the left touchline, his path blocked by a wall of Newcastle defenders. So he turns inside and fires a high ball square across the field to where Tommy Smith is moving up. Tommy doesn't even bother to bring the ball under control, but simply flicks a gentle volleyed pass to Brian Hall outside. Smith, as Liverpool players do, moves after he has passed, Hall sees his run and feeds him. Tommy turns on the ball, sees Steve Heighway moving towards him on the edge of the area and plays it in to him. Again Smith is on the move as soon as he has passed, and Heighway knocks the ball back into his stride. Smith reaches the by-line, pulls the ball back low and firm through to Keegan for a tap-in.

But no sooner had the celebrations for this second FA Cup win died down than the club and its fans were hit by a massive hangover. That summer Bill Shankly announced his retirement, citing a 'pressurised job' as one of his reasons for going. Smith recalls his reaction to the news: 'We were all shell-shocked. But when the dust settled you knew that he'd left behind a fortress that wasn't going to be conquered in any shape or form. It was unfortunate that Shanks should have had a little bit of a problem with the directors, and he hung around a bit not knowing what do with himself. Used to turn up at Melwood for training, which was a bit embarrassing for Bob Paisley who'd taken over. Shanks probably had too much influence over the side in the following season, 1974–75, when we won nothing.'

But even in this first post-Shankly season, Liverpool only lost the title to Derby County by two points. Poor away form, with only 16 goals scored, probably made the difference. There was some problem accommodating Ray Kennedy, Shankly's last signing, who spent most of that season vying with John Toshack for the number

10 shirt. But throughout the turmoil, Tommy Smith ploughed on as reliable as ever, ensconced in the right-back position as if he'd been there all his life.

He did, however, produce one hilarious cameo in the away leg of the European Cup-Winners' Cup tie against Ferencvaros. As he went to take a throw, a bottle flew from the crowd and hit him on the shoulder. At first he shrugged it off but then, I suspect, the possibility of winning the tie in a UEFA committee room occurred to him, as he suddenly fell to the ground as if mortally wounded. The performance was not convincing, though, and Ferencvaros went through on the away goal they'd scored at Anfield.

Halfway through the 1975–76 season, the boot-room finally solved the Ray Kennedy problem by moving him to the left side of midfield, and the team began to tick again. 'Bob got it sorted out,' Tommy remembers, 'because he was about to prove he was a great manager in his own right. He didn't really have to put anything else in place except maybe one or two players.'

Among these were two new full-backs, Phil Neal and Joey Jones, both of whom started the season as first choice, with Smith confined to the bench or to the reserves. Emlyn Hughes had taken over the captaincy. But yet again Tommy bounced back, as Jones was soon dropped, Neal switched to left-back and Smith reclaimed his number 2 shirt, to complete 24 games of the league programme. Liverpool were pushed right to the wire by an unlikely challenge from Queen's Park Rangers, but Liverpool's improved away form – only three defeats – helped keep them ahead. They had to win at Molineux in the last game to seal the Championship, and though Steve Kindon put Wolves ahead, a huge throng of travelling support urged the team on to success, with the three goals coming in the last 14 minutes. Liverpool had the title by a point.

It was even closer in the final of the UEFA Cup. Liverpool had lost only one leg – 1–0 away to Hibernian in the first round – on their way to the final, with perhaps their best result being the 1–0 win away from home at Barcelona (a Toshack goal) in the first leg of the semi-final. The home leg was still a tense affair, because the Catalan club had two Dutch Johans in their line-up, Cruyff and

Neeskens, who had both played in the World Cup final two years earlier.

Despite the nerves he induced, it was great to see Cruyff back at Anfield eight and a half years after he'd thwarted us with Ajax. I was squeezed up against the wall in the paddock – it was a full house of over 55,000 that night – torn by the conflicting desires of wanting to see a great player perform well, but still finish on the losing side. In the end I more or less got what I wanted. Barcelona were probably the better team, but could only manage a 1–1 draw – Phil Thompson scoring from close range for us, Carlos Rexach getting theirs – allowing the Reds to go through 2–1 on aggregate.

I couldn't make it to the first leg of the final, as I had no money for the fare home. To make things worse, I spent the night baby-sitting for the writer Neville Smith, the man who wrote a play about Everton forward Alex Young entitled *The Golden Vision*, who was highly chuffed to go out for dinner with Bruges leading Liverpool by 2–0. But Nev was distinctly smirkless when he returned to find that Liverpool had scored three second-half goals. A 1–1 draw in Belgium was enough to complete a second 'double' for the club, and give Tommy Smith his seventh major honour.

But the reinstatement of Joey Jones at the beginning of the 1976–77 season really did see Smith relegated to the bench as stand-in for Phil Thompson, who was prospering in the centre of defence, while the full-backs Neal and Jones were virtually ever-presents. Smith managed 16 League games, mostly when Thompson was out with a cartilage operation, as Liverpool edged out Manchester City – this is not a printing error – by one point to take another title. The likes of Terry McDermott and Jimmy Case were jostling for regular places, knowing that Kevin Keegan was playing his last season for Liverpool. Perhaps it was this internal competition within the squad that pushed the team to new heights, for by the end of April 1977 they had won through to both the FA and European Cup finals, and a remarkable treble was still possible.

Because of Thompson's injury Smith was right in the thick of things, playing from the sixth round onwards in the FA Cup, through to that fatal moment when Lou Macari's corner-flag-bound shot deflected of Jimmy Greenhoff's chest to give United their classic winner in the Cup final, denying us, at a stroke, both the Double, and a treble. Our one retrospective consolation was that the victory allowed Tommy Docherty to manage United for a few more months.

Meanwhile, Tommy Smith's contributions to the European campaign proved to be more fruitful. He was certainly a handy man to have around when Liverpool had to play in eastern Turkey against Trabzonspor, who were backed by a fanatical – in the original sense of the word – following. He remembers looking out of the dressing-room window before the match and seeing police baton-charging the fans in an attempt to quell their fervour. But human rights were the least of his worries.

'It was a terrible trip. The khazi at the hotel was just a hole in the floor, with no toilet-paper, and you could have a shit, a shower and a shave all at the same time. The dressing-room at the stadium wasn't much better. The grass on the pitch was over your ankles. We lost 1–0 to a penalty, but it could have been a lot worse.'

Fortunately the home leg was rather more comfortable, despite the presence of about 12,000 Turks at the Anfield Road End. (For some reason my diary fails to reveal why I was at the game – not having any work in London might have had something to do with it.) The Trabzonspor supporters made a hell of a noise for about an hour before the kick-off, but then Liverpool scored three goals inside 20 minutes, and that was it – apart from some late kicking by the Turks which, perhaps fortunately, Tommy was not on the pitch to sort out.

When the spring came round, Smith was only on the bench for the away leg against the brilliant French champions, St Etienne. Although he came on for the injured John Toshack during the match, which Liverpool lost 1–0, he already had it in mind to retire, after sensing that his time with the club was over. 'I'd been out of the team, or on the bench for the best part of the season, and I'd had enough. I was just going to pack it in. I told the people at the club and they understood. I had my testimonial game coming up in May, anyway, and the club rule was that you didn't play on after that.'

But with both Toshack and Thompson ruled out for the season, Smith was moved from back-up to front-line to historic effect. Wednesday, 16 March 1977, at Anfield is a date seared on the memory of most supporters of a certain age. The second-leg quarter-final against St Etienne had everything – a huge crowd, made more colourful by vocal French support; a dramatic start; a traumatic middle; and a cathartic climax.

When Keegan's hopeful cross sailed into the top corner to level the tie inside two minutes, my brother, who was sitting alongside me in the Kemlyn Road stand, grabbed my face with such intensity that he nearly ripped my head off. I was trying to work out whether Tommy Smith, who had moved in towards the cross, had got a touch. He hadn't, but his run may well have distracted the French goalie – a defender joining the attack in the first minutes, *mon dieu!*

The match bubbled with excitement and good football almost from start to finish. When Dominique Bathenay battered an equaliser in the second half, Liverpool needed two goals to win on aggregate. The French had an away goal – so it had to be 3–1 or bust. Ray Kennedy put Liverpool 2–1 up on the night, before substitute David Fairclough created the biggest noise I've ever heard at a football ground by scoring the winner eight minutes from time.

Liverpool brushed FC Zurich aside in the semi-final, and were booked for Rome against what had become regular rivals on the Euro-circuit, Borussia Moenchengladbach. It was definitely going to be Keegan's last game and, so it seemed, Tommy Smith's too. Fourteen years after his début, at the age of 32, the man who'd been at the heart of Liverpool's rise to power had the biggest stage of his life for his departure.

It is a measure of all great footballers that they can summon the will to control their destiny, and that of the team around them, when the occasion demands it. Diego Maradona did it for Argentina in the 1986 World Cup, so did Pele for Brazil in 1970, and Beckenbauer in 1974, but not, sadly, Johan Cruyff. On 25 May in Rome, both Keegan and Smith achieved theirs in different ways. Keegan's all-action performance might have been expected. But Tommy Smith heading in from a corner to put Liverpool 2–1 ahead?

'It couldn't have happened better. It was my 600th game for the club, and the last. It had been planned for me to go up for corners, because we didn't have much height up front without Tosh. I can only guess that the Borussia defenders took one look at me and thought they wouldn't have to worry about an old feller, so when Stevie Heighway's corner came in, spot on, I had a free header. After the game me and Ian Callaghan had a little word together, about this finally making up for the Inter Milan defeat in 1965. It did – but you couldn't help wondering what might have been.'

Smith returned to Liverpool to massive celebrations, which spilled over into his benefit game at Anfield two nights later. But instead of bowing out, he was offered yet another year at the club, so iconic had he become.

So as Alan Hansen, Kenny Dalglish and Graeme Souness arrived to form a new generation of great Liverpool players, they brushed shoulders with one of the true originals. Hansen played alongside Smith, both in the league and in Europe, that season and recalls his impressions of the senior player: 'It's a misconception that Tommy was only a hard man. He was actually very good on the ball. If they'd got both of us at our peaks, I think the partnership would have been well nigh perfect. He was the type of player that never gives up. I remember we were alongside each other for a few games, one of which was Steve Ogrizovic's début in goal at Derby County. Anyway, we're 4–0 down, I'm having a nightmare, and I'm wishing I'm on my way home, on the bus. But Tommy's still trying. He won't let it go. I mean, he's trying harder at 4–0 down than when it was 0–0. If I'd played with him for longer I'm sure some of that attitude would have rubbed off on me.'

It was, I suppose, both ironic and yet apt that Tommy should succumb to an injury just before the 1978 European Cup final against Bruges at Wembley, and be replaced by Alan Hansen. It was somehow typically Tommy Smith to do a lap of honour on crutches before the game, a showman and a professional to the last. 'I still got a winner's medal, you know?' he smiles, before slipping away, his right leg bearing a pronounced limp from all the tackles.

Nowadays, Tommy hosts the letters page in Liverpool's *Football*

Echo, agreeing with many of the points the grumblers make about the latest generation of Liverpool player. You almost wish he could be turned loose in the current dressing-room before games to remind them of their obligations to the fans, but the club has no official role for him. So, instead, he does the circuit of sporting dinners, making speeches about his past – how he was in the first Liverpool team to win an FA Cup, how he was the first Liverpool captain to lift a European trophy, how he scored a goal that helped win our first European Cup, and why he still can't stand Emlyn Hughes.

PETER THOMPSON

The White Pele

This may sound like something from *The X Files*, but I promise you it's true. On Saturday, 23 November 1963, the day after President John F. Kennedy was assassinated in Dallas, Liverpool won 1–0 at Manchester United with a headed goal by Ron Yeats, his first for the club. That victory put the team on top of the First Division – and this is the spooky bit – for the first time since 1947 when the club had last won the league.

I discovered this weird fact in the programme notes for the home game against Burnley on Saturday, 30 November 1963, while studying the Liverpool career of Peter Thompson, the flying left-winger who was one of our best players ever and who, to my 11-year-old eyes, seemed to epitomise 'cool' before it could ever be applied to football. With his neatly parted hair and squared-off sideboards, he was as stylish as Patrick 'Danger Man' McGoohan or even Steve McQueen. The clothes he wore off the pitch – suede jacket, white turtle-neck sweater – displayed the first stirrings of mod fashion in football, bringing together two of the three passions with which our gang was utterly fascinated. Our starch-collared headmaster even issued a diatribe in assembly one morning in 1963 against this cultural wave lapping at the foundations of his world of conformity. Tab-collared shirts and button-downs were out, and instant detention awaited any boy turning up with the flashiest item, a shirt with a little gold bar pulling the points of the collar together. Grey mohair slip-overs were not allowed, Cuban heels were totally forbidden and anything suede would be impounded. No identity bracelets, no signet rings, no coloured socks, no excessively large centre vents artificially cut into our blazers. But, even as he spoke, the look on his face suggested that he had already lost the battle.

To us Peter Thompson represented a first victory of style over uniformity, not only in the way he looked, but also in the way he played. He was our George Best, but was better than that because he stayed and he delivered.

Meeting Thompson as a 55-year-old man and seeing that he retains all his style was a heartening experience. He still dresses well, and if it's a cliché that many footballers from the 1960s ended up running pubs – partly because they never got to earn the big money, partly because their social horizons were not allowed to expand – it is typical of Peter Thompson that the 'pub' he now owns is a beautiful whitewashed hotel in the tiny Lakeland village of Bowland Bridge, watched over by the Cartmel Fells.

The Hare & Hounds Country Inn is stylishly appointed, but then you wouldn't expect anything else from the man who, in August 1963, turned up to sign for Liverpool wearing a devastatingly well-cut sports jacket and white trousers, and driving a white sports car (even though that had been borrowed from a friend). The pictures in the *Liverpool Echo* of Peter Thompson arriving at the club, being mobbed by fans, were as one with anything they could show of Billy J. Kramer, a Beatle or one of The Searchers, who had just had a number-one hit in the charts with 'Sweets For My Sweet'. But the welcome committee had shrewdly been tipped off, as Thompson remembers with a broad smile.

'I couldn't work out what all these people were doing outside Anfield when I came to see Bill Shankly,' he says. 'There must have been about a thousand or so, with press and photographers as well. I made my way through to the entrance where Bill was waiting and I asked him what was going on. "They're all here to see you, son, if you sign for me today!" I was completely fascinated by him. He took me round Anfield and gave me the talk that I later heard him give to lots of other players he was trying to impress, about what an honour it would be to play for Liverpool. I then made a terrible mistake in the meeting by bringing up the subject of a signing-on fee, which a business partner of mine had put me up to. Shankly went white with anger. "I'm giving you the chance to play for the greatest team in the world, and you want illegal money! There's a flaw in your character, son. Now get out!" And I panicked, so I quickly grabbed hold of the pen and signed, which was the best thing I ever did.'

Thompson, though, had already enacted, albeit unwittingly, his own 'trick' on Liverpool. In February 1962 his former club Preston North End had knocked Liverpool out of the FA Cup in a second replay held at Old Trafford, after holding them to two goalless draws.

Thompson wasn't supposed to play in the game, having been injured, but was pressed into service: 'I think I kidded Shankly there. Preston had lost 3–1 at home to Liverpool in the league, and it could have been ten. It was embarrassing. But the same team somehow managed two draws and in the second replay it was snowing, I wasn't playing very well, and then the ball dropped out of the sky, I swung a leg and the ball flew into the net and we'd knocked Liverpool out.'

Preston may have had luck on their side in the Cup, but they were relegated from the Second Division that season and an ambitious young Thompson, who'd been an England Schoolboy International, soon had an eye on a move. Born in Carlisle, he'd played for the town's schools team after developing his prodigious dribbling skills from the age of five onwards – no doubt inspired by those famous Lancashire wingers of the 1950s, Stanley Matthews of Blackpool and Tommy Finney of Preston, whose club signed the teenage Thompson to the groundstaff in August 1958. Although a member of Preston's team for the 1960 FA Youth Cup final, Thompson soon found that the club had little potential for his development.

'At 20 I was classed as a "has-been wonderboy" by the local press. I was a winger, but at Preston where we were getting beat 4–0 and 5–0 every week, I could never get out of my own half. So when Liverpool came in for me, I jumped at the chance, especially when Shankly said to me, "I don't want you in our half, Thommo, only in their half, attacking." It was music to my ears. I was ambitious, and I wanted to win things.'

Thompson duly signed for Liverpool in August 1963 for a fee of

£35,000, on a basic wage of £50 a week plus win bonuses, which seemed a lot of money to Thompson, whose dad was an £11-a-week joiner. He went straight into the first team, who had battled their way to eighth place in their first season back in the top division, but who plainly needed strengthening if they were to challenge for honours.

But they won only one of their first four games (2–1 away at Blackburn Rovers), losing twice at home, to banish most thoughts of immediate success. As Thompson settled, however, the team began to flourish. He scored his first goal for the club in a 6–0 thrashing of Wolves; and his second, a few games later, came in a 5–2 win over Aston Villa. Thompson's dashing style of wing-play – he would always seek to attack the right-back and get past him as soon as he got the ball – triggered an apposite response from Roger Hunt and Ian St John, who would end the season with 31 and 21 goals respectively, with reserve striker Alf Arrowsmith also claiming 15 goals in just 20 appearances, and the overall team total reached a whopping 92.

Thompson played in all 42 games that season, scoring only six goals – 'the biggest disappointment of my career was that I never scored enough' – but two of those came in the dramatic win over Arsenal which clinched the Championship. They were typical Thompson efforts, both fierce right-footed shots after cutting inside from the wing towards the penalty box, hit on the run with great power, in the 52nd and 57th minutes of the match. Arsenal were routed 5–0, and Liverpool celebrated. Nick Hornby, Rory McGrath, Tom Watt, Melvyn Bragg: your boys took one hell of a beating that day!

In fact, Thompson's only mistake of a spectacular first season was in having the wrong-coloured car. 'Bob Paisley came up to me after training one morning and told me Shanks wanted to see me. I was a bit worried, and Bill looked very serious. "I'm very disappointed in you, Thommo – you've got a blue car! You're playing for Liverpool not Everton, so get rid of it!"'

Thompson quickly obliged his boss, taking a £200 loss on the incriminating vehicle, but at least buying himself a bit of peace and quiet in the passionate but unpredictable world of Bill Shankly. This was probably best revealed at the Melwood training ground where Shankly and Bob Paisley – at that stage coach and physiotherapist – had set up routines which are still serving the club to this day. Their success was at the heart of the club's progress to international fame, yet outsiders are still baffled by the effect such apparently simple methods have wrought. One part football training, two parts manipulative psychology, they were formulated by the two men's shared values, by their hard upbringings in mining communities, by wartime experience and by their own footballing careers of the 1940s and '50s. Peter Thompson gives valuable insights into the formula in its early stages of evolution.

'There was absolutely no coaching. Training was mostly five-a-side games mixed with shuttle-runs which were meant to imitate the stop-and-start nature of football. We were running 10 yards and back, 20 yards and back, 30 yards and back. After an hour of this, your legs had buckled. We'd just sit down on the grass exhausted and Shankly would come over and say, "Hello, boys, how are you feeling?" I remember one morning when a lad said that he was knackered and Shanks just exploded. "Knackered? You've trained for one hour, you're going back to a beautiful house in a fabulous car, it's a beautiful day, and you're knackered? Get down the mines for a week, then come back and tell me you're knackered!" He almost had the lad in tears. So the next time he asked us how we were, we all said we weren't tired and he exploded again. "Christ! Bob Paisley, come here – these boys haven't done enough work, they're not tired!" So he made us start all over again and do another hour!'

Thompson also remembers the times Shankly joined in the five-a-sides, pushing, shoving and swearing his way to the ball, barking out, 'Are you a winner?' to individual players as he tackled them. 'I only want winners' was another mantra, followed by 'Second place is no good to me'.

If Melwood sounds more like a boot camp than a training centre at this time, it should be said that Thompson is wreathed in fond smiles as he retells these stories, dropping into his fair impression of Shankly's growling voice whenever the memory summons a phrase from the past. And he acknowledges that the players could hardly complain about their lot.

'We'd report to Melwood at 10.30 a.m., train for an hour or so, have a meal, and then we'd have the afternoon off. And everywhere you moved in Liverpool, everyone wanted our autographs. The likes of Cilla Black, Jimmy Tarbuck and Gerry Marsden used to come down to the ground. When you went out, there were always people coming over to your table, offering to buy you drinks or food. And, best of all, we were winning. The first year I was there we were Champions, the second we won the FA Cup, the third we were Champions again, and the fourth year we finished fifth. That's when Shanks called a crisis meeting! It was a lovely place to be.'

Thompson's first season was made even lovelier when he was retained in Alf Ramsey's England squad for a summer tournament in Brazil in 1964. He had won his first two international caps early in May (a 3–4 win against Portugal in Lisbon and a 1–3 win against Ireland in Dublin) and now he was jetting off, via New York, to display his talents in Rio de Janeiro and São Paolo.

England beat the USA 10–0, with Thompson's Liverpool team-mate Roger Hunt scoring four goals, but the results in the Brazil tournament were less satisfactory. They lost 5–1 to the hosts, drew 1–1 with Portugal and were narrowly beaten 1–0 by Argentina. Nevertheless, Thompson had acquitted himself well, and had received a 'good press' both locally in Brazil and, to borrow a phrase, 'back home'.

'It was a smashing spell for me, and I came back with rave reviews. I popped into Anfield because I knew that even though it was summer Shanks and Paisley would be there. Bill greeted me with open arms and said, "Christ, Thommo, they're calling you the white Pele! Can you believe that? You're the white Pele!" Of course a few weeks later, when the season started, I was right off form, couldn't get going at all, and Bill called me into his office. "Everyone said you were the white Pele, son, now you're playing more like the white Nellie!" But that's the way he worked. He could boost you up and make you feel so important, but if he thought you were on a high horse, you could bet he would knock you down.'

Thompson's poor start to the 1964–65 season was – cause and effect? – mirrored by the team's. They lost five of their opening eight league games, including an embarrassing 4–0 home defeat to Everton. It wouldn't quite be true to say that the Champions declined to defend their title, but by the end of 1964 they had won only eight of their 24 league games. By then, though, Liverpool seemed to have acquired a taste for the more exotic, as they breezed through the first two rounds of the European Cup, winning all four legs, including the emphatic 3–0 home win over Anderlecht. But as the year turned, the new momentum given by the European campaign started to deliver the goods domestically. Liverpool won five league games on the trot, and by the end of February they had reached the sixth round of the FA Cup, after a minor scare with a home draw against basement club Stockport County in the fourth round.

During March, Liverpool finally saw off Cologne in the European Cup quarter-finals after three drawn games, when skipper Ron Yeats called the right colour for the toss of a disc that would decide the tie. They had also defeated the hated Leicester City 1–0 at Anfield after a replay to leave the club in the semi-finals of both the FA Cup and the European Cup.

Thompson recalls this dizzying spell in the club's fortunes, as they attempted to win two trophies, more or less at the same time: 'Shankly was a great motivator, but he wasn't so hot on tactics, as I think most ex-players of the time will tell you. I mean, we had meetings where he had 13 or 14 players down on the team-sheet because he'd miscounted. But Bob Paisley was something of a tactician, and a good learner too, so it was a good partnership to take us through all these games. We were a bit lucky to get past Cologne on the toss-up. That was very late on a Wednesday night in Rotterdam, and on the Saturday we had the FA Cup semi-final against Chelsea at Villa Park. We had to travel back overnight from Germany and then get ready to go down to Birmingham, and Shanks just said to us, "Don't say you're tired. That word is not in my vocabulary!" Chelsea had all these young stars coming through – Bobby Tambling, John Hollins, Terry Venables, George Graham –

and we thought we might get the runaround. But we kept it simple, as instructed, and they didn't see much of the ball. Then I went on a bit of a run, got outside their right-back and hit a left-footer between Peter Bonetti and his near post to give us the lead. Willie Stevenson scored a penalty near the end and we were through to the final.

For those who think the football authorities of today are bad planners, it may be some comfort to know that they were just as incompetent 30-odd years ago. The FA Cup was scheduled for Saturday, 1 May 1965, with the two legs of the European Cup semi-final against Inter Milan fixed for Tuesday, 4 May, and Wednesday, 12 May. Meanwhile, Liverpool were left to slog through their ten remaining League games between 1 April and 26 April. Alex Ferguson would probably self-detonate in similar circumstances.

Needless to say, Liverpool were not at their best in these games, winning just three and losing five to finish an inconsequential seventh in the division. Fears that this drudgery would take the edge off them for the FA Cup final were proved half right. Played in showery, strength-sapping conditions, the game staggered its way into extra-time before headers by Hunt and St John beat Billy Bremner's volley to win Liverpool the Cup for the first time. Thompson was pleased at the achievement, but disappointed in his own contribution.

'I had a poor game that day, one of the worst in my career. I always liked to put on a bit of a show, but I had trouble with Leeds' right-back Paul Reaney. He was a smashing defender, a very quick lad, strong too. I'd seen him mark George Best out of a couple of games too, so maybe I was in good company. But it was one of those days when you had to take satisfaction in what the team did, and I was thrilled to bits that we'd won.'

The team celebrated that night at the London Hilton before travelling back up to Liverpool on the Sunday for a massive reception from the fans. By Tuesday tea-time 54,000 of us were crammed into Anfield to watch Liverpool take on Inter Milan. Whatever weariness they felt from the demands of the Cup final had been more than offset by the euphoria of winning the trophy. It seemed to the crowd, not to mention Inter, that Liverpool were almost insanely committed to attack. Peter Thompson confirms that impression.

'It was a fabulous night. Hardly anyone had been able to score against Inter because of the defensive system they played, but there we were, 3–1 up against them. Chris Lawler had also scored a fantastic goal, but it was ruled out because Geoff Strong was supposed to have been offside. We also hit the bar and the post. Shanks had asked us to attack them, with Cally [Ian Callaghan] and I taking on the full-backs from the start. He wanted us to keep it simple, though, which in my case probably involved taking four on instead of six! My style was that of a "jinker" while Cally was more of a straight-line, speedy runner. If we found ourselves struggling against a full-back, Shanks would let us swap over, which is what we did a few times that night against Inter. They just couldn't cope with us. But Shanks always encouraged me to go past people, to take them on. When I got picked for England Ramsey said, "I want you to play the same way as you do for Liverpool, but don't hold onto the ball." What was I supposed to do then? But Shankly never in ten years asked me to change my style. Against the Italians he was up and down the touchline shouting, "Thommo! Get past him!"'

Helenio Herrera, Inter Milan's coach, admitted after the match that 'We have been beaten before, but tonight we were defeated.' Eight days later, however, it was a different story for all sorts of reasons, not least being the fact that Peter Thompson was called away on England duty on the weekend between the two legs, flying to Belgrade where England were playing a friendly against Yugoslavia. Thompson wasn't picked for the team after falling ill with a stomach bug, which left him enfeebled by the time he flew from Belgrade to meet up with Liverpool in their Lake Como hotel.

'I spoke to Bill and Bob Paisley when I arrived and told them I'd be fit to play, but I don't think I was really 100 per cent. We also had a disturbed night before the game. I was rooming with Cally, and we were fast asleep when Shanks burst in and said, "Can you hear these bloody church bells, boys? They're keeping everyone awake! You can't sleep with this racket going on. I've moved you." So we had to move up four floors, and of course then we couldn't get back to sleep. Cally and I were wide awake for ages, just talking. When it came to the match, there were 90,000 in their stadium, with flares being set off. We got off to a bad start, losing an early goal. We also made the mistake of attacking them rather than trying to defend our lead. And they were dubious goals, theirs, which was all a bit sad. I'm sure that Liverpool team would have handled it all a lot better in a couple of years time because there's an art in dealing with Europe. I know that Bob Paisley and the lads in the boot-room learnt lots of things on that trip which they used later to our advantage.'

Liverpool had played 59 competitive matches that season using a core of just 11 players, backed up by four or five reserves. For 1965–66 Shankly refined this apparent wastefulness to the same 11 players plus Geoff Strong, an all-purpose player signed for £40,000 in November 1964. Nine of the chosen 11 played in 40 League games or more. But then, as Thompson remembers, 'You could go 50 or 60 games without injury, but then if you missed one Shankly would call you a hypochondriac, and he'd be deadly serious.'

Thompson missed the first two games of that season as Liverpool sought to get back to what Shankly termed 'our bread and butter' – winning the Championship – but played through the season thereafter. His confidence in his playing style had been boosted by England recognition and by the encouragement Shankly gave him. 'I was obsessed with my football, it was my whole life,' he cheerfully admits, as he became the one major individualist in a team dedicated to a collective pattern of play. 'When they made some of the five-a-side games one-touch only, I couldn't bear it, because I hated giving the ball away.'

But Thompson's consistent ability to take on defenders, to get past them with his dribbling skills and his pace, and to get crosses in from the by-line, reaped rich dividends for the others players, notably Roger Hunt, who scored a remarkable total of 30 goals in the 37 games he played. Thompson remembers the euphoric effects that winning had on the team.

'There was a super spirit in the team, and a superb atmosphere in the dressing-room. Because of our successes, the pressures any manager feels from the board to get results were lifted, so it was a bit like being in Butlin's. We played five-a-sides all the time and Shanks would come to training beaming all over, saying, "Hello, boys, what do you want to do today?" and we'd say, "Five-a-side," and he'd walk away and leave us to it. I was enjoying my football so much that before one game Willie Stevenson asked Shanks for two balls, one for the team and one for me!'

Liverpool beat Manchester United 2–1 at Anfield on New Year's Day 1966, and went unbeaten in the league until the end of February, losing 2–0 at Fulham of all places. But they then lost only one more game, 2–0 at Burnley, and took the title by six points from Leeds United. A third-round Cup exit, losing 2–1 at home to Chelsea, probably helped concentrate minds on the two remaining trophies.

The European Cup-Winners' Cup brought them to the brink of their first continental trophy, with Thompson contributing a rare goal in the 3–1 first-round home-leg win over Standard Liège of Belgium. Juventus had been beaten in the preliminary round (some preliminary!), and the spring saw us ease past Honved of Hungary and then Celtic in the semi-final. Thompson, scything down the right wing, set up Roger Hunt's equaliser in the final against Borussia Dortmund but, in an uncanny foreshadowing of what would happen in the World Cup final in July, the ball looked to have crossed the by-line before Thompson centred it. 'I've seen it on video,' Thompson says with a shrug, 'and it looks at least a yard over. The linesman flagged then put it down when the referee gave the goal.' Liverpool's luck then rebounded on them with Dortmund's flukey winner in extra-time.

But Thompson, Hunt, Ian Callaghan, Gordon Milne and Gerry Byrne were at least consoled by their call-up to Alf Ramsey's 28-man squad for the World Cup. As the deadline loomed to finalise the chosen 22, however, Thompson began to feel a dread about Ramsey's professed disregard for specialist wingers: 'I'd played 11 games on the trot for England in the run-up to the World Cup, but then in the last couple of games Alf left me out. I was getting married that summer and I had word with Ramsey about it, but I didn't really expect him to say I was definitely in at that stage. So I had a week's honeymoon and joined up with the squad, did all the training and then one day Alf started walking round the pitch talking to individual players. He had to leave six out, and he'd told five of them before he came across to me. "Am I one of the six?" I asked, and he nodded and said sorry. I was terribly disappointed. I'd started to feel like I'd made it, because we were all getting fitted out with suits and shirts, boots and tracksuits. And that morning we'd all been given white macs. The six of us were invited into his office and asked if we had any questions and "Budgie" Byrne of West Ham just asked if he could keep the mac.'

Thompson suffered an identical fate four years later when he was included in the 28-man squad for Mexico as the only winger, but half-expected that he would be left out again: 'It wasn't such a disappointment second time around, but I couldn't help wondering what a winger might have done after seeing what Grabowski did for West Germany in that game against England, when he came on and turned the game round for them.'

Between his two World Cup disappointments, Thompson continued to play with great verve for Liverpool. In the 1966–67 season he gave a glimpse of what 'winged wonders' could achieve, scoring ten goals as an ever-present. Like most of his strikes, spectacular shooting was a feature, and there were two particularly memorable thunderbolts against West Ham in January 1967, which just happened to be recorded for posterity in an episode of *Till Death Do Us Part*, as Alf Garnett and his 'Scouse Git' son-in-law attended the match at Anfield.

But Liverpool's form tailed off dramatically in the spring and I remember standing forlornly in the rain at the last game of the season as relegated Blackpool came to Anfield and won 3–1 in front of a sour crowd of just 28,000. With Ajax blasting us out of the European Cup and Everton beating us 1–0 in the fifth round of the FA Cup, it was certainly a season of anticlimax after three years of thrills and success. Season 1967–68 wasn't much better, but we went close in 1968–69 as Thompson contributed eight goals and a constant stream of good performances to help us to the runners-up spot behind Leeds. The 1969–70 season was all about the Watford defeat – a game Thompson was grateful to miss – and its consequences: 'I was never into tactics, I was an individualist, so the decline in the team wasn't obvious to me. That's why I run a pub now, rather than being a football manager. I couldn't have been a manager. So I didn't know what was going wrong; we were always threatening but just couldn't get our hands on another trophy. Maybe they were a bit late bringing in new players – Emlyn Hughes was the only new lad that really broke into that team – but I still don't know why those players, including myself, who'd been so successful, suddenly weren't. One of those things, I suppose.'

Thompson survived Shankly's culling of older players after Watford, and came on as substitute in the 1971 Cup final against Arsenal, but had gradually begun to succumb to the wear and tear on his legs which his twisting and turning, not to mention the opposition's tackles, had wrought. And an injured player, as he knew only too well, was likely to be frowned upon by Shankly.

He recalls an FA Cup replay at Leicester City – yes, them again – in 1970 when he was pressed into playing with a dodgy hamstring, as Paisley and Shankly did their famous good-cop/bad-cop routine on him before the game in order to convince Thompson that he was fit. On a terrible, wintry pitch he eventually went down in agony as the hamstring snapped, and retreated to the quiet of the dressing-room, whereupon Shankly appeared to berate him.

'"You betrayed me!" he shouted. "You lied to me! You said you were fit! You're a con-man, Peter Thompson!" A swearing match followed as the game went on outside, and then suddenly there were roars from the crowd at the Liverpool end. Alun Evans had scored for us. Shanks disappeared, and then Evans got another in the last minute. When the team came back in I was feeling pretty sorry for myself, but Shankly came over and put an arm round me and called for silence. "I want to thank this man Peter Thompson. He has played as a cripple tonight – for me, for my wife Nessie and for the people of Liverpool!"'

For all the relish Thompson shows for the anecdotal legacy Bill

Shankly bequeathed to him – and which forms the core of his occasional speeches at sporting dinners – there is no disguising his sadness that the relationship between them deteriorated as Thompson's potency waned in the early 1970s.

'Shankly was funny. He'd treated me like a son, and I was obsessed with him. But once I'd had cartilages out of my left knee, and Steve Heighway got into the team, it was like he didn't need me anymore. It was different, and he was a bit odd with me. I went for a month on loan to Bolton and Jimmy Armfield wanted to sign me, and I told him that Shanks would probably let me go for nothing. But when Jimmy asked, he was told they wanted £20,000 for me, which was a lot of money for a player with a gammy knee. But Shanks insisted he couldn't let an international go for nothing, even after ten years. So I signed for Bolton and I asked Shankly if he'd bring a team to play in my testimonial one day. He'd played 16 years for Preston and never had a benefit game, which had always hurt him, but he looked at me and said, "We'll come and play for you, son."'

Five years later, even though Shankly had resigned by then, Liverpool kept their word and brought the 1977 European Cup-winning team to Bolton to pay tribute to a player who'd helped lay the foundations for that victory. 'It was my last game, so it was a nice way to finish,' Thompson says wistfully.

Though Thompson had always been more business-minded than most players of his generation – he once owned a petrol station on the road behind the Kop – the adjustment to normal life proved to be difficult.

'When it's all over it takes a long time to get the game out of your system. Playing football and training was all I did between the ages of 15 and 35, so when I found myself sitting on a tractor running two caravan parks I'd bought near Blackpool I was pretty unhappy for a while. I was okay money-wise, and I had a wife and two kiddies, but it was really hard to accept that it was all gone. What you miss most is not so much the playing but the patter and the jokes you used to have in training. But it's okay now, I can go back to Anfield and enjoy a game, and I've got something out of it. There was no financial advice in my day, partly because when you're 20 you think being 30 is an old man, and partly because the club wasn't really that bothered. I've had a lot of players come in here since I finished and it's a bit sad because they're really struggling. When it's all over, you're a has-been, and you have to stand on your own two feet. Now players earn so much money they should be able to cope when they finish.'

Peter Thompson has more than coped. He has a thriving business, a baby daughter by his new wife, a healthy tan and a leanness which suggests he could still give Vinnie Jones a run for his money. He keeps many of his Liverpool souvenirs and England caps in a discreet cabinet in a corner of The Hare & Hounds, so that those visitors who know about his other life can share some memories, and that those who don't can find out if they want to.

And he has two other little souvenirs which he carries around with him – scars on his legs, which show up as white marks when he's sun-bathing. One is called 'Paul Reaney', the other 'Norman Hunter', as tributes to their creators and the many battles he fought with them in the 1960s.

'Luckily, they didn't catch me enough times to put me out of the game . . .'

RAY CLEMENCE

England's Number One

When Liverpool fans first caught sight of new goalkeeper Ray Clemence, there was an unexpected novelty about him – he was slim. From the end of 1962 onwards we had grown used to seeing the rather chubbier figure of Scotsman Tommy Lawrence in goal, his green jersey rolling up whenever he dived to make a save to reveal a tyre of white flesh hanging over his shorts. He was nicknamed, with typical Scouse bluntness, 'The Flying Pig'. Tommy was still a good goalkeeper, good enough for Shankly and for Scotland, but because of his perceived weight problem there was a slight comic undertow to his performances. With his big bush of unkempt dark hair and his rolled-up sleeves, you could imagine that he'd spent the last half-hour before a game having a pint and a ciggie in the local pub before turning out. There was one classic joke about him, which has been used against other corpulent keepers since, and it concerns a penalty he failed to save in front of the Kop. As Lawrence collected the ball from the net, a voice in the crowd is supposed to have shouted: 'Hey, Tommy – if that had been a pie, I bet you'd have saved it!'

Ray Clemence was never likely to face such heckling, although when he made his first-team début in a League Cup third-round tie against Swansea Town at Anfield on Wednesday, 25 September 1968, he remembers hearing a singular hostile voice about his performance.

'It was a wicked, awful night. There was a gale force wind and it was lashing down with rain. And in my early days at Liverpool I had a problem kicking the ball off the floor and had to spend time in training improving my technique. In the first half of that game I was at the Anfield Road End, and the wind and the rain were blowing right in my face, so I didn't get one ball off the ground from my goal-kicks. At times Swansea were just shooting wide because they knew that as I took a goal-kick they were getting the ball straight back. I remember one Scouser behind me shouting, "Clemence, take an early bath, will you, you're useless!." I often wonder if that bloke still remembers what he did, given what I achieved with the club afterwards.'

Despite the heckling, Clemence managed to keep Swansea out that night as Liverpool recorded a 2–0 win with goals by Chris Lawler and Roger Hunt. It had taken him over a year to get this first senior appearance, having signed for the club from Scunthorpe United for £18,000 during the close-season of 1967. He had been watched several times by Shankly, who was initially suspicious about Clemence being left-footed. But several convincing performances by the young goalkeeper led to a fateful phone call, while Clemence was spending the 'Summer of Love' handing out deckchairs on Skegness beach.

'I was only on £11 a week with Scunthorpe in the off-season, so I had to find something to do to bring extra money in. It was a nice job, sitting on the beach in the sun – sometimes! One day I had a message sent down from the council offices asking me to ring home immediately, and my parents told me the club had been on, needing to speak to me urgently. I called them and they told me they'd accepted an offer for me from Liverpool, if I was interested. And there was absolutely no doubt that I was. The following day, I was driven across to Liverpool by one of Scunthorpe's directors in his Rolls-Royce, and met the great Bill Shankly. The was no doubt I was going to sign, no matter what the financial terms were. I think he knew that anyway but it didn't stop him giving me the big sell. He took me down to Melwood to see what he called the "greatest training ground in the world", around Anfield, which was the "greatest football ground in the world" and up onto the Kop, where the "greatest supporters in the world" stood. He took me out to lunch at the Lord Nelson Hotel, and brought me back to his office. I just took the contract and signed straightaway.'

Of course, Shankly wouldn't be Shankly if there wasn't a twist somewhere. He had intimated to Clemence in discussions that if he kept on improving as rapidly as he had been doing at Scunthorpe, he would be in the first team within six months, because Tommy Lawrence was supposed to be coming to the end of his career. But a surprise was waiting for Clemence when he reported for pre-season training, because it soon became obvious that Lawrence was far from finished, wasn't coming up to 30 years of age as Shankly had said, but was, at 27, at the peak of his career. Not for the first time a player had fallen for a little touch of Shankly's kidology. But Clemence was happy enough in spite of this.

'It meant me being a little bit patient; but, having said that, I was pleased I had those couple of years in the reserves – with the two first-team games – because it gave me a good grounding, it made me realise what the club was about, what pressure you had to play under, and it gave me a chance to learn the particular way a Liverpool keeper had to play, which at that time was totally different to any other goalie in the league. You had to be a sweeper as well as a goalkeeper, it was as simple as that.'

In those days, of course, there were few goalkeeping coaches, which meant that Clemence had to learn from watching and talking to Tommy Lawrence, and adding that to what he had picked up as a youngster from Scunthorpe's veteran goalkeeper Geoff Sidebottom, who had also played with Aston Villa and Wolves, and who basically taught Clemence how to look after himself in a time when forwards had greater licence to put their shoulder in on opposing goalkeepers.

These days Clemence sits in the air-conditioned comfort of his Football Association office, surrounded by walls of match video-tapes and all the other accoutrements of the modern football era. His role as a specialist goalkeeping coach for the England team is a fair distance away from his early days at Liverpool, and the significance of the journey is not lost on him.

'The game has progressed so much, really. Certain goalkeepers these days do have advantages that some of us didn't. What I had at Liverpool was Tommy Lawrence's experience. For me, he was the best keeper around in one-versus-one situations; very rarely was he beaten in that sort of scenario. His timing was superb, he always stood up and made himself a big figure, so he taught me that side of it – not necessarily by taking me out and working with me, but by us talking and me watching him. And when I made my break-through into the England squad, I was lucky enough to have Gordon Banks still around, so I could talk and work with him as well.'

The 'sweeper' role that Clemence inherited and refined at Liverpool basically involved him patrolling the edge of the box, ready for the ball over the top that might catch the Liverpool back four pushing up at the wrong time. The other element that he brought into modernising the Liverpool team's goalkeeping was the early throw. It was very nearly his trademark in the 1970s: the save or the catch of the cross, followed by the instant throwing out to a full-back or midfield player who had already started to make space and move forward.

'It was part of the philosophy at Anfield then – and it's coming back now – that goals were easier to score on the counter-attack than when you had your opponents penned back under pressure. A team can be at its most vulnerable the moment the ball changes sides, so if we got the ball quickly and attacked the opposition as quickly as we could, we'd have a better chance than if we took 90 seconds or so to move the ball upfield. The first thought was to pass it quickly, but if that wasn't possible we'd keep possession and wait for the opening. It never involved me kicking the ball long.' (Author's note: I think Steve Heighway scoring Liverpool's second in the 1974 FA Cup final, after John Toshack had flicked on a mighty Clemence kick, may have been an exception!) Clemence played one more game after his début against Swansea, another home cup-tie, the FA Cup this time, against Wrexham in the fourth round, on Saturday, 24 January 1970. Liverpool won 3–1, thanks to two goals from Bobby Graham and one from Ian St John, and when Liverpool beat Leicester City in the fifth round the omens looked good for a trip to Wembley. But nemesis, in the unlikely shape of Watford's Barry Endean, loomed. Clemence watched this fateful game from the bench and thought that 'Tommy Lawrence played well, despite getting some of the blame for the goal'. In the dressing-room afterwards, however, Shankly made both his anger and his intentions clear, as Ray remembers clearly.

'Everybody inside the club had expected us to get past Watford and into the semi-finals, and Shanks certainly wasn't happy, you could tell that. He'd always been a great believer in sticking with his men, knowing that if they had a bad game they'd usually come back from that. But his feeling was that this was one bad game too many.'

The following week, Tommy Lawrence, Ron Yeats, Ian St John and Ian Ross were all dropped, as Peter Thompson and Tommy Smith returned and Doug Livermore and Ray Clemence were brought in. Ironically, the team lost 2–0 at home to Derby County, but Clemence was in to stay, completing the rest of the season in the green jersey.

The following season he played in all bar one of the club's league games, conceding just 22 goals, despite having to work with a defence being reconstructed around newcomers Larry Lloyd and Alec Lindsay. Clemence also appeared in all ten of Liverpool's European Fairs Cup matches, letting in only four goals, one of which was the Bremner effort at Anfield which knocked Liverpool out in the semi-final.

The new goalkeeper also kept clean sheets all the way to the FA Cup semi-final, until conceding one – to Alan Ball – in the 2–1 victory at Old Trafford. Liverpool's young team were in the Cup final, facing Arsenal, and it seemed as though Clemence might finish his first full season with a winner's medal.

'We felt there was a lot of promise in the team. We'd had a reasonable season together, and it was magnificent for us to get to the Cup final. I felt okay all week, I felt fine going to Wembley, all right in the dressing-room and all right in the tunnel. But as soon as I walked out out of that reasonably quiet tunnel and the hundred thousand voices and bright sunlight hit me, I think for the one time in my career that if I could have turned back down the tunnel I would have done so. The occasion was all too much for me. I can remember most things about games, but I've seen the goals in this one a million times and I still can't remember anything about the game, because it just came and went. All I remember is sitting in the bath afterwards, feeling terribly disappointed, but also worried that I'd played in an FA Cup final and couldn't recall anything about it other than that we got beaten. I thought I might never come back here again, because most players never even get one chance to play at Wembley let alone two.'

Clemence's anxieties were eventually laid aside in 1974, with the 3–0 win over Newcastle, 'one of the most one-sided Cup finals in history'. And in the previous season the youthful promise of the team had finally been fulfilled in dramatic style with the league Championship and the UEFA Cup double.

Clemence played in 41 league matches, missing only the game at Derby County with a thigh strain. There, his unfortunate deputy Frankie Lane did little to harm Clemence's chances of a quick return by scoring an own-goal, stepping back over the line after he had caught a cross, to help Derby to a 2–1 win, one of only seven defeats for the Reds that season.

In the UEFA Cup Clemence was in commanding form, culminating in what proved to be one of the 'two most important saves of my career'. Liverpool were already 3–0 up in the re-staged first leg of the final at home against Borussia Moenchengladbach (who boasted the talents of Berti Vogts and Gunter Netzer) when the Germans were awarded a late penalty, and the chance of a vital away goal. But Clemence plunged low to his right to beat out Josef Heynckes' spot-kick to preserve the three-goal advantage. Confirmation of just how vital that save had been came in the return leg when Moenchengladbach stormed into a 2–0 first-half lead, before Liverpool rallied to keep them out. Had the penalty gone in at Anfield, the Germans would have had the Cup on the away-goals rule. So Clemence's save effectively won Liverpool their first European trophy.

Three pots in two seasons – the league, the UEFA Cup, and the FA Cup – confirmed that Shankly had built another great team and, as Clemence remembers, the overriding feeling was one of relief: 'We were still a young side, and for years we'd had it thrown at us that we'd never be as good as the 1964–66 team, but now we had an extra belief that we could go on to even better things.'

Like all the players, Clemence had fallen under the spell of Shankly, which only turned malign when it came to the question of injuries: 'I remember twisting my ankle in training the day before an away game at Newcastle, and at a normal club they'd probably have agreed that I had no chance of being fit. But Shanks insisted I travel on the coach with the team, wearing a carpet slipper, with my ankle swollen up like a balloon. About an hour or so before the game he made me take a fitness test, which I technically failed but he just said, "You'll be all right, son, get out and play." So I wore one boot a size bigger than normal on my injured foot, and fortunately I didn't have a lot to do and we won. But you'd probably lose count of the number of Liverpool players of that time who went into games carrying injuries. I think it was his wish that we should all have a high pain threshold. If you were ever in the treatment room at Anfield he used to pop his head round the door, not his body, look at anybody in there, and just shake his head and walk out. You knew he was not best pleased.'

Despite this Spartan régime, the Liverpool players held Shankly in the greatest affection, which made his decision to quit in the summer of 1974 a complete shock: 'They say everybody remembers were they were when Kennedy was killed, and it was the same with the news of Bill's retirement. Shanks was a charismatic bloke and a fantastic motivator while always trying to keep the game simple.'

Nevertheless, the senior professionals at the club, among whom Clemence was emphatically now a member, instantly rallied around Bob Paisley when he was accepted by the board as Shankly's chosen successor, and it was business as usual for the team. They'd finished second to Leeds, five points adrift, in 1974 and were runners-up again in Paisley's first season, this time two points behind Derby County. Clemence was an ever-present in both seasons, and was so again when they became Champions for the fourth time in the modern era in 1976, having beaten off a sustained challenge by QPR to win by just one point. Liverpool's defence was a key factor that season, conceding only 31 goals and losing just five games.

Clemence recalls his own role, which extended to more than just making brilliant saves: 'I set high standards defensively, in terms of us all knowing the jobs we had to do. If one of the defenders or midfield players wasn't doing his job, I'd tell him about it, it was as simple as that. And they'd tell me in return. That was the sort of team spirit we had. There were a lot of strong characters but, in saying that, we all got on well and accepted that if you got a rollicking from a team-mate, it wasn't just for the sake of it but because you hadn't done something which you should have done.

'So, yes, on a Saturday I'd be very vociferous throughout the game, and there were many times when I'd come off the pitch without having had any saves to make, but I'd still have a sore throat and a severe headache from the shouting and the sheer concentration of watching the defence. All that information I was giving to defenders was meant to stop the ball from getting to me. I was just naturally competitive. Even in the five-a-sides in training, when I played up front as a forward, I just hated to lose. You can't accept that it's not your day today, that you'll just come back tomorrow. I think if you're going to be a winner that has to be in your make-up. I still hate to lose now – golf, the England team's games, anything.'

The Championship success in 1976 was again twinned with another UEFA Cup victory, with Liverpool losing only the first leg of the first-round tie at Hibernian, then going unbeaten throughout the rest of the tournament. A 3–1 win away against Real Sociedad, was followed by a thumping 6–0 home win. Slask Wroclaw were seen off 5–1 on aggregate and Clemence produced another of his special penalty saves away to Dynamo Dresden to set Liverpool up for a 2–1 aggregate victory. Barcelona were beaten in the semi-final, and the comeback from 2–0 down to Anfield against Bruges to a 3–2 win proved enough of a psychological blow to hold off the Belgians 1–1 in the return leg of the final. Liverpool had their second European trophy.

For most football clubs, it would have been tempting to sit back and reflect on their triumphs, but Liverpool, right from Shankly's early days, had always adopted a 'tomorrow we start all over again' attitude after any success. The subtle changes that Bob Paisley had made to the team had established both a consistency of style and a hard-core squad of first-teamers who more or less picked themselves. Phil Neal had come in at right-back, and Phil Thompson and Emlyn Hughes were now established as mobile, ball-playing centre-backs, with Ray Kennedy as a left-sided, attacking midfield player, and Jimmy Case as the tough-tackling guardian of the right flank. Meanwhile, the gangling but charismatic Welsh left-back Joey Jones had attracted the attention of Paisley as well as the Kop. Up front, the Toshack-Keegan-Heighway partnership seemed as potent as ever.

'We had some excellent players at that stage, intelligent players too, who'd always been willing to learn from other games, especially in Europe,' recalls Clemence. 'In November 1973, for example, we'd been knocked out of the European Cup by Red Star Belgrade, who'd basically given us a lesson in passing and movement over both legs, but particularly so at Anfield. Our players looked at what had happened and decided we could do that as well, because we had players who were comfortable on the ball in all areas of the pitch. Bob Paisley and the back-room staff at Anfield were also capable of making subtle changes – maybe just by having a word with certain players without the rest of the squad necessarily being aware of it. It was a constant process of improvement. So, once we'd got players who were comfortable on the ball playing in the centre of defence – Phil Thompson and Emlyn Hughes, and later Alan Hansen – there was always the option for me just to roll the ball to one of them, and they would start movements from there.'

Liverpool's accumulated European experience finally paid off in that remarkable 1976–77 season. It wasn't just in terms of the sophistication they could bring to their play, but also their ability to conduct games at a tempo of their own making. That season eventually consisted of 61 competitive games, and to win both the league and the European Cup, and finish runners-up in the FA Cup, required both stamina and patience in order to last the distance.

I can probably accept now, 20-odd years later, that Liverpool didn't actually have the most difficult of draws in the European Cup that year – Crusaders and Trabzonspor in the first and second rounds and FC Zurich in the semi-final were certainly ideal picks, when the likes of Real Madrid, Torino, Dynamo Kiev and Bayern Munich were lurking around. But that doesn't detract from the team's achievement in beating St Etienne in the quarter-finals – 'The biggest noise, the best atmosphere ever at Anfield,' Clemence says – nor from Liverpool's winning performance in the final itself.

Everyone who has ever had even a mildest interest in the club will have distinctive memories of that night in Rome's Olympic Stadium on Wednesday, 25 May 1977. My own are fogged by the fatigue of the two-day train journey, the hygiene consequences of wearing the same replica Liverpool shirt for over 50 hours non-stop, the afternoon's modest drinking, the long, hot walk out to the stadium, and the sheer amount of throat-stripping shouting and singing that all of the 26,000 Liverpool fans generated throughout the game. The ecstasy of victory was quickly dissipated by the need to get back to the chaotic district railway station for a return journey that wasn't as much fun as, say, staying in Rome overnight for fine wines, a few hours in a club, and a celebratory champagne breakfast in bed. But then I was completely potless at the time.

Ray Clemence's summary of the same evening is understandably more euphoric and succinct – 'It was the greatest night, ever!' – but in the specialised world of a goalkeeper's game, it was also the night that Clemence made the second of the 'two most important saves of my career', he mentioned earlier. Most Liverpool fans use one word as a reference for this – 'Stielike!' (which is not a German exclamation relating to a sudden bowel movement but the name of the Moenchengladbach midfield player who, at a vital point in the match, had the ball at his feet and only Ray Clemence to beat to put the Germans into the lead). Okay, I was lying about the bowel movement – Stielike generated 26,000 of them in those clammy few seconds, which Clemence remembers in almost forensic detail.

'We'd played really well, we were 1–0 in front through Terry Mac, but then we'd made just one error, and [Allan] Simonsen punished us for it. And having just lost the FA Cup final on the Saturday, we suddenly had a nervy ten-minute spell after their goal when we lost our way a little bit. That's when Stielike had this chance, and if it had gone in I'm not that sure we'd have picked ourselves up enough to actually go on and win it. But, thankfully, I managed to get in the way of it, and we went on from there. I just did what I'd done so many times before in the past when I was faced with a one-on-one situation. First, I always tried to get myself into the right position. Second, I'd make myself look as big as I possibly could. And then third, when he was about to strike the ball, I'd try and spread myself towards the ball and hope that he'd hit me with it, which is exactly what Stielike did! It happened many other times in my career, but that was probably the most important block I ever had to make.'

That night in Rome marked the end of the brief but memorable Kevin Keegan era at Liverpool. In just six seasons he'd helped inspire Liverpool to win three league Championships, an FA Cup, the European Cup and two UEFA Cups. Clemence says that 'Kevin just ran Berti Vogts ragged that night, and Berti was supposed to be the best marker in the world at the time. It was a great way to sign off.'

For Clemence, though, it must have seemed that there were no peaks left to conquer, except for the fact that the Liverpool philosophy after winning a trophy was to go straight out and win it again. And they did just that in 1978, easing past Dynamo Dresden (6–3 on aggregate), Benfica (6–2), poor old Borussia Moenchengladbach again (4–2) and then beating Bruges 1–0 in the final at Wembley. The winning goal was scored by Kenny Dalglish from a pass by Graeme Souness, and Liverpool also had Alan Hansen in defence that night. The 'Three Jocks', as they called themselves, would be an essential part of the most successful Liverpool team ever – and we'll be hearing from them soon – but Clemence wasn't finished yet.

Graeme Souness, arriving at Liverpool as a player with a burning hunger for achievement, immediately recognised that the Liverpool goalkeeper, despite his success, was of like mind: 'Clem was a fantastic competitor – on the pitch, in training, wherever. He absolutely hated to lose.'

The alchemy created between the new Scottish trio and the rest of the team was truly magical. Although they couldn't defend their

European crown for a third time – falling to the eventual winners Nottingham Forest in the first round – the Liverpool team of 1978–79 produced probably their most crushing Championship performance in beating off Forest by eight points, losing only four games all season. What's more, for Clemence in particular, there was an epic dimension to the triumph, as he and his defence conceded only 16 goals in 42 games.

'I would like to think that it's one record that will never be beaten. We had a very special side. We only conceded four goals at home all year. We felt we were unbeatable. People may say, when you've only conceded so few goals, that you must have been a defensive side, but we scored 85 goals that year! We were just a very, very good side who, from a goalkeeper's point of view, were magnificent to play behind because everyone was a defender when we needed it, and everyone was an attacker when that was required.'

Translating Liverpool's 30 wins and eight draws that season into the three-points-for-a-win system, would give them 98 points. Three of the defeats were by a 1–0 scoreline – away at Everton, Arsenal and, bizarrely, Bristol City – while Aston Villa where the only team to score more than a goal against Liverpool, winning 3–1 at home in April 1979. Clemence played in all 42 games and kept a clean sheet in 28 of them. It is no coincidence that six of the men I selected for this book played in this team – Clemence, Alan Kennedy, Alan Hansen, Graeme Souness, Kenny Dalglish and Terry McDermott.

Clemence won another Championship medal the following season, missing one game to allow Steve Ogrizovic his début, but Liverpool were knocked out in the semi-finals of both the FA Cup and the League Cup, to Arsenal (after three replays) and Forest respectively.

We didn't know it at the time – and nor did he for that matter – but the 1980–81 season would be Clemence's last as a Liverpool player. He was in his prime, he and Peter Shilton couldn't be separated as England's first-choice goalkeeper by the manager Ron Greenwood, and the Liverpool team was on the point of unleashing Ian Rush on a football world which was already beginning to wave the white flag. But after a first-ever victory in the League Cup final, beating West Ham 2–1 in a replay, and a third victory in the European Cup, 1–0 against Real Madrid, Clemence suddenly knew that it was over.

'It just became a situation which happens in all walks of life. We'd won the European Cup final, against Real Madrid in the Parc des Princes. You couldn't get a more glamorous game than that. And as I came into the dressing-room afterwards, there was champagne everywhere, photographers and television cameras everywhere, and I just sat in the corner with my glass and looked at it. I should have been like everybody else, dancing around and shouting, but I was sat there thinking, "I've seen all this before." It just wasn't giving me what normal wins used to. And so I made a decision there and then that for me to get the best out of myself for the rest of my career, I had to go and face a new challenge somewhere else. I'd won five Championships, three European Cups, two UEFA Cups and the FA Cup – I'd won everything there was to win in the game. I was 31, going on 32, and I needed a new push. I'd also seen many other great Liverpool players, because it was such a fantastic club, staying on so long that their last move would often be to a club where they could never win anything. And I didn't wanted to be in that situation, just seeing out my time as a player. I wanted to be competing and trying to win things.'

By leaving when he did, Clemence effectively missed out on another sideboard's worth of trophies won over the next six seasons, but has no apparent regret about his decision. 'It's easy to look back and think I might have won this or won that, might even have been still involved with the club, but you make decisions in life and you have to stick by them.'

When Clemence returned to Anfield with his new club Tottenham Hotpsur in May of the following season, it was an apt occasion in every way. Liverpool needed a win to make sure of another Championship, so Clemence received a rapturous salute from the Kop, followed by a second-half battering from his former team-mates, who put three goals past him – Mark Lawrenson with a header, Dalglish with a low left-footer inside the box, and Ronnie

Whelan with a thumping left-foot volley into the top corner of the net. And all in front of a triumphal Kop.

After 14 years at Anfield, Ray Clemence had finally found out what it must have been like for the hundreds of other goalkeepers who'd stood in front of the Red tide, and lost.

Return of the Mac

It says a great deal about Liverpool Football Club, and probably something about Terry McDermott too, when he reveals that 'all the time I was at Liverpool, I never felt I was a regular; I always felt as though I was just two games away from being dropped'.

This feeling of insecurity, coming from a man who was later to be named Footballer of the Year, gives further insight into the competitive nature which both Bill Shankly and Bob Paisley cultivated in the various squads under their charge. As we have seen, Shankly used a form of psychological warfare to ensure that his players left all but the most serious of injuries unacknowledged. The fear of incurring his displeasure, of being thought a weakling, and of losing their place in the team, propelled players to exert mind over body.

With Bob Paisley, the technique was slightly more subtle and the preferred target was individual form and confidence rather than injury, although as a fully trained physiotherapist he had a specialist's insight into whether a player was malingering or not. Allied to the mind games he deployed on his players was the permanent and genuine sense of competition for places within the squad. Paisley regularly, and shrewdly, bought players to make sure that those already at Anfield knew they were only as a good as their next game, and that any sense of self-congratulation would be short-lived.

Initially, Terry McDermott was one such player, signed in November 1974 for a modest £175,000 just months after playing for Newcastle United in the Cup final against Liverpool. Bill Shankly had already signed Ray Kennedy from Arsenal as his last act before resignation, so you can imagine how a Cup-winning team might have reacted to two new buys coming in so soon after an easy victory – they tried harder, which was exactly what Paisley wanted.

So Terry McDermott's sense of impermanence was partly a consequence of the manager's style. It was also probably to do with his own sense of self-worth. Born and bred in Kirkby, a vast post-war housing development on the northern edges of Liverpool which had a reputation for being the toughest area of Merseyside, he had played for the town's schoolboy team, dreaming of joining the Liverpool team he supported from the Kop. But, as Terry recalled in between mouthfuls of shepherd's pie and orange squash after a heavy training session at Newcastle's Maiden Castle sports complex, it didn't happen.

'We had a good team at the time [late 1960s], but I was one of the lesser lights. The best player was John McLaughlin whom Liverpool signed, while a couple of others went on to Bolton Wanderers. The last two to get picked up by professional clubs were me and Dennis Mortimer, which was a bit ironic since we both ended up going further than the rest. [Mortimer captained Aston Villa to the Championship in 1981, and then to their European Cup victory in 1982.] At the time it didn't bother me too much because I was just a kid from Kirkby who wanted to play football. I didn't pass any O-levels or anything, I didn't even study, as such. Obviously the Liverpool and Everton scouts had watched our games but couldn't have seen much in us. Makes you think about how so many footballers are late developers. Anyway, the only club to come in for me was Bury. I was out at an evening match at Anfield, Liverpool versus Burnley I think it was, and when I got home the Bury scout Colin MacDonald had been round and left forms for me and Dennis. I signed that night, while Denis held off and eventually went to Coventry City.'

Terry made his début for Third Division Bury as a substitute in the game against Stockport County in January 1970, when presumably you could have got longish odds on him scoring a goal in a European Cup final that decade – even longer when Bury were relegated to the Fourth Division in 1971. But he must have been doing something right, because Newcastle United, in Division One, came in for him in February 1973, paying Bury £25,000.

'I'd heard they were interested in me, and I'd heard Liverpool had been looking at me but nothing had materialised from them. I was a wing-half, playing on both the right and left sides, mainly doing the midfield tackling. I was a different type of player then to what I became at Liverpool. Anyway, we were due to play Reading and Newcastle's manager, Joe Harvey, was coming down. But, lo and behold, the game was fogged off about an hour before kick-off. But they still took me, on the word of their chief scout.'

Terry's career had taken a sudden upward move at long last, but the really fateful event, which so often dictates a footballer's career, happened in the 1973–74 season when, out of the blue, Newcastle produced an FA Cup run which took them all the way to Wembley. Terry's part in this was to score three goals – one in the third-round replay against Hendon, another in their nervy 1–1 draw at home to Scunthorpe in the fourth, and the third in the bizarre sixth-round tie at home to Nottingham Forest which was abandoned after a pitch invasion with Newcastle leading 4–3. The match was replayed twice at Everton's ground, with Newcastle finally beating Forest 1–0, and then easing past Burnley 2–0 in the semi-final. Terry was thrilled to find his favourite team waiting for him at Wembley on 4 May.

'It was just unbelievable for me. Even playing them in a league game had been a thrill. They still had players I'd watched from the Kop – Chris Lawler, Tommy Smith, John Toshack, Emlyn Hughes – and I'd never dreamed I'd be on the same pitch as them one day, let alone at Wembley. Obviously, I wanted Newcastle to win, but the next best thing was for the Reds to do it, which of course they did. I think the 3–0 scoreline flattered Newcastle a bit on the day. Liverpool were just all over us. Gave us a lesson.'

Nevertheless, amid all the turmoil over Shankly's departure in the summer, new manager Bob Paisley and his scouting team must have had McDermott's name logged: 'Maybe they'd been watching how I played under pressure, and an FA Cup final's certainly pressure, with all those people watching on telly. You still have to keep playing even when you're 3–0 down.' Whatever Liverpool had seen was enough to make them buy McDermott early in November, with the places of Brian Hall and Peter Cormack coming under pressure. John Toshack was also out injured for a lengthy spell. So after Liverpool had lost 3–1 at home to Arsenal on Saturday, 9 November 1974, and then 1–0 at home to Middlesbrough in a League Cup tie the following Tuesday, Terry McDermott was immediately signed and went straight into the team for a quiet introduction in the Merseyside derby at Goodison Park. A goalless draw was played out in front of nearly 57,000 fans. Terry Mac was back. He was photographed for the next home game programme – against West Ham on 23 November – standing next to Ray Kennedy in front of the 'This Is Anfield' sign in the players' tunnel. Fashion experts should note that at this point in his career, Terry was sporting a pre-perm pudding basin haircut, the moustache was barely growing, and his sweater had a pattern on it that looked like television interference.

The picture at Anfield was no clearer, with the fans wondering how the team would cope without their great guru, and Bob Paisley feeling his way into management. The results had been patchy, with November turning out to be particularly bad, as the team failed to register a single win in five games. They also went out of the Cup-Winners' Cup in the second round to Hungary's Ferencvaros on the away-goals rule, and the League Cup by losing at home to Middlesbrough on 12 November. When they lost 3–1 at Birmingham City just before Christmas, Terry was dropped after just six games, a blow made worse by Liverpool's immediate return to form with a 4–1 home win over Manchester City on Boxing Day, with two of the goals coming from the restored Brian Hall. Competition. It was the start of a tough time for McDermott; he played only eight more full games that season, although he did achieve the consolation of his first league goal for the Reds in a 1–1 draw at Burnley, and then scored his second in a 4–0 home win over Newcastle United.

But the overall impression McDermott created was that his bandy-legged, elbow-waggling running was better suited to lower divisions than the Elysian fields of Anfield. Liverpool had finished second in Paisley's first season, and as the manager himself admitted, 'For anyone else that would be fine, but for Liverpool it's not good enough.'

Nevertheless, Terry McDermott started in the first seven games of the 1975–76 season – won three, drew two, lost two – before being dropped again, this time to the extent that he only made two further league appearances, as a substitute, in that Championship season, and he didn't feature at all in the club's successful UEFA Cup campaign. At times like this the Liverpool way did not embrace pastoral care. 'You took your medicine, turned out in the reserves, played your bollocks off, and if you were lucky word went up that you were ready for the first team again, should anyone in it be off form or injured.'

McDermott remembers feeling that his brief Liverpool career might have come to an end. 'I struggled for two years, no question about that. I wasn't playing well, and I lacked confidence. Looking back on it now, there were times when I felt I should be in the team, but mostly I didn't deserve to be playing first-team football. At one point I went in to see Bob Paisley to have a talk, and told him I wanted to leave. I was getting the same money in the reserves as I was for the first team, but I wanted to play football. He said I should stay in the reserves a bit longer while he had a think, because he didn't actually want me to go. The best thing that happened to me, though, was that Roy Evans, who was the reserve-team coach at the time, gave me a lot of encouragement and helped me get my confidence back. He was the one who kept my chin up. He used to say, "Keep playing your football, keep enjoying it, and you'll be back. They want you here, you know, because you've got ability." All of which helped me knuckle down to fight for my place.'

Through Liverpool's epic 1976–77 season, McDermott gradually worked his way back into the first team, running up his longest unbroken sequence of appearances from the end of March as the team advanced on three major trophies – the League, the FA Cup and the European Cup. 'I felt more a part of the first team than at any other time during my first two years,' McDermott says. His spectacular goal against Everton in the drawn FA Cup semi-final at

Maine Road gave convincing evidence both of his return to form and of his goalscoring virtuosity. Taking a Kevin Keegan pass on his right foot just outside the Everton area, he threw off an Everton challenge by turning inside and then unhesitatingly curled a wonderful left-foot chip over keeper David Lawson. And although he missed the dramatic European Cup home tie against St Etienne, he played in both victories over FC Zurich in the semi-finals.

I'm no tactical genius, but it did seem that having Jimmy Case playing as the midfield player outside him freed McDermott to make some of the instinctive runs from deep which were soon to become his trademark. It was, of course, one of these which enabled him to latch onto Steve Heighway's astute pass and hit it first time to score Liverpool's first goal in the European Cup final against Moenchengladbach in Rome.

'We should really have won the Treble, because we were an outstanding team. We were the better side against Manchester United in the FA Cup final, getting beat by a jammy goal. But we showed our true character by going to Rome and winning, right after the massive downer of losing a Cup final. And it was a great performance too, because the Germans were no mugs – they had internationals all over the park. Not many teams could have done that. Nothing was said between the two games; there was just the switch of bringing in Ian Callaghan for David Johnson because Bob felt we should have more bodies in midfield. I've got a clear memory of the goals, but the game itself is a bit of a blur. I'll certainly never forget the sight when we came out into the Olympic Stadium about an hour before kick-off and saw those 26,000 Liverpool fans there. It was unbelievable – just a sea of red and white. There was just no way we could lose that game, because we knew how much Liverpool people must have spent to get there.'

Terry McDermott's part in Liverpool's historic victory ought to have brought him peace of mind for the coming season, but even now he stills seems to think that he wasn't quite a regular at the time. Of course, Liverpool were now in the early stages of another of their subtle yet vital metamorphoses. The Keegan era was over, Kevin having decamped to SV Hamburg in the summer, and Kenny

Dalglish had arrived from Celtic to take over the number 7 shirt, if not quite the same role that Keegan had played. There were doubts about how much longer Tommy Smith and Ian Callaghan could last, and John Toshack's Liverpool career was coming to a close. So it would be a season of gradual change before another settled side emerged.

Despite McDermott's sense of insecurity, there was no doubt that Paisley had seen a role for him in the new team, and he played in the first 11 league games, notching a couple of goals along the way. It took until the second leg of the European Super Cup – a typical piece of UEFA confection involving two matches between the winners of the two senior European competitions, deep into winter – for Terry to start to feel good about his chances, however. He scored a brilliant hat-trick in the 6–0 thrashing of Keegan's new club Hamburg at Anfield on 6 December 1977 to give Liverpool a 7–1 aggregate, and the Kop a chance to gloat at Keegan, a touch unnecessarily, with a chant of 'Liverpool re-ject, Liverpool re-ject, hel-lo, hel-lo!'. McDermott remembers only the good things to come from the match: 'John Toshack went on telly after that game and said something nice about me, how I'd now proved myself to be an important part of the team, and so maybe subconsciously that gave me another lift, because it came from a respected player, and the goals obviously helped me as well.'

It is now time to reveal a minor coincidence, which is that Terry McDermott and I were both born on the same day, 8 December 1951. It's no big deal, but astrologists might wish to note that my own career, like Terry's, had begun to look up in the latter part of 1977. I was getting a slightly better class of freelance work out of *Time Out*, as skateboarding reports had now given way to a feature based on six weeks spent training and travelling with league new boys Wimbledon; also, a half-hour play that Andrew Nickolds and I had written in our spare time, *Hold the Back Page*, was recorded at BBC Pebble Mill in mid-October; and we'd got commissions for a *Crown Court* from Granada, and an episode of Terry Venables and Gordon Williams' detective series *Hazell* from Thames Television. Three and half years of avoiding a 'proper job', and thereby a proper wage, suddenly seemed to have been justified. But I should point out to the star-charters that, unlike Terry, I had not scored in a European Cup final that year. Shortly afterwards, yes . . . which is a good point to stop trying to force a parallel between my fellow Sagittarian McDermott's career, and my own.

Even for a pessimistic Terry McDermott, 1977–78 turned out to be pretty good after all. He missed only six league games, and helped Liverpool reach the League Cup final against the rising team of the moment, Brian Clough's Nottingham Forest (who also went on to win the Championship) to whom we lost 1–0 in a replay at Old Trafford, thanks to a dodgy foul by Phil Thompson and a dodgy penalty award from the referee. But Liverpool retained the European Cup by seeing off Dynamo Dresden, Benfica (Terry scored in the 4–1 home victory) and poor old Moenchengladbach again, before beating Bruges 1–0 in the Wembley final, with a goal from Kenny Dalglish, provided by Graeme Souness's pass. With Alan Hansen coming into the team, a strong Scottish presence had been established through the centre of the side, in defence, midfield and attack. Bruges were pretty cautious on the night – 'it wasn't a classic' is Terry's curt summary – but Liverpool had their name on that huge bulbous cup for a second time, and this time I had enough money for a proper celebration, which I recall involved driving down Park Lane in a car loaded with six other Liverpool fans, shouting at completely bemused Arab tourists.

Despite this second wave of success, McDermott confirms that there was no change to either Anfield's low-key style of management, or to the dressing-room's collective ego. 'They had no qualms about leaving anyone out of the team if it was the right thing to do, and there was certainly no star system in the dressing-room. If we had superstars, they were out on the pitch, in the public eye, but there was nothing like that among the team. Nobody was bigger than anybody else. It was the same with Kenny as it was with Kevin – nobody asked for any special treatment, and nobody got it. So there was great camaraderie and team spirit, we had a will to win, we knew we were the best and proved it on numerous occasions. And if we ever got slaughtered in the press, pre-season or whenever, that was just the incentive we needed to go out and win some more trophies.'

The 1978–79 season was no less epic for Terry McDermott than it was for Ray Clemence, Alan Hansen, Kenny Dalglish, Graeme Souness and the other ten players used for the first team that year. Everyone could take pride in their own contribution to a magnificent season, and yet could still enjoy the contributions of others. Terry, like all the midfield players contributed to the team's 85-goal total with eight of his own (Ray Kennedy scored ten, Souness eight, Jimmy Case seven), with the most memorable arriving on Saturday, 2 September, as Liverpool thrashed Spurs – and their new signings Ossie Ardiles and Ricky Villa – 7–0 at Anfield. Dalglish had already scored two, as had David Johnson, while Ray Kennedy and Phil Neal with a penalty, soon made it six. Fourteen minutes were left when Liverpool cleared a Spurs corner and . . . 'The header?' McDermott remembers, laying modesty and forgetfulness aside for a moment. 'Now I *do* remember that goal.'

Spurs have a corner on their left in front of the Kop, and when the kick drifts aimlessly to the far side of the penalty area, Liverpool pounce. Ray Kennedy heads the ball clear, Dalglish picks it up, turns and passes it forward to David Johnson, who controls the ball and changes direction virtually all in one movement, before sweeping a pass with the outside of his right foot into Steve Heighway's path on the left wing. Heighway crosses first time to the far post, where McDermott arrives to head into the top corner past the unfortunate Barry Daines. Terry had been back in his own area defending the corner, and the time from Ray Kennedy's clearing header to the ball hitting the Spurs net is just on 13 seconds. So how did Terry McDermott do it, and why?

'I just don't know. I can't put me finger on it at all. It must just have been instinct. I was on the post defending the corner, so why did I run from there to end up at Tottenham's far post? I don't know. We were 6–0 up, so why did I bother? I just don't know. I get baffled by it some times when I look back. I suppose it must have just been confidence, and a bit of inspiration.'

Terry shared penalty-taking duties with Phil Neal that season, further evidence that his days of self-doubt were over, and one of his penalties helped beat Champions Nottingham Forest 2–0 at Anfield in December, with McDermott also getting the other goal. It was a small but vital revenge for Forest knocking us out of the European Cup after the two had been drawn to face each other in the first round. And although Liverpool put together a decent FA Cup run, advancing to the semi-finals, it was Manchester United who did for us in a replay at Goodison Park after the teams had drawn 2–2 at Maine Road. It seemed a drag then, because that team was certainly worth the Double, but there was some small compensation in the exquisite torture of Alan Sunderland's late winner for Arsenal in the final, after United had pulled two goals back to equalise.

In fact we had achieved a rare double over United that season anyway, winning 3–0 at Old Trafford on Boxing Day, and then 2–0 at home on 14 April. Around about this time, my fortunes and Terry's varied somewhat. He scored two goals in a Liverpool run of five straight wins while my grandmother died on Friday, 6 April. The following day I went to a friend's funeral in Oxford, and then my father died the next day. When I returned to match action at Villa Park on Easter Monday, we lost 3–1, and my trousers caught fire after somebody tossed a dog-end onto them. So much for astrology. Or perhaps not . . .

In conversation with Terry, it emerged that *The Sun* had offered the Liverpool team £50,000 that season if they met the paper's challenge of scoring 84 goals (i.e. two a game) or more. 'I think we had to play Leeds in the last game. We were on 82 goals beforehand. We got one [from David Johnson] but then the referee disallowed a Jimmy Case goal and we all started going demented, surrounding the ref like maniacs. He couldn't believe what was going on, because we'd already won the league. Couldn't see what the fuss was all about. But we got there in the end, winning 3–0.'

Of course, there was no suggestion that what was to become Merseyside's least favourite newspaper had influenced the Liverpool players into such free-scoring form. If that had been true, clubs would have been sacking their managers and replacing them with a sack of money behind the desk, as a means of team motivation.

What it was, I suppose, was a combination of another competitive element dangled in front of a team who hated losing at anything, and a typically cunning stunt from Rupert Murdoch's department for publicity. But it wasn't *The Sun* wot won it.

Liverpool won the Championship the following season in a slightly less convincing manner – but then it would have been impossible to have been *more* convincing than '79 – scoring just 81 goals this time around, and giving the others a chance by conceding a carefree 30. They missed out on another potential Double by losing to Arsenal in the *third* replay of an FA Cup semi-final that had become so protracted it was eventually played on a Thursday night at Coventry City's ground just nine days before the final itself. Brian Talbot headed the winner, but in the final at Wembley West Ham this time defeated the club who had had the temerity to thwart the Mighty Reds. It was still a pity because Terry had scored one of his greatest goals in the sixth round at Tottenham to win the tie, receiving the ball wide on the right then flicking it up and volleying a dipping shot into the far top corner of the Spurs goal. 'I don't know why I did that one either,' Terry muses. 'Glenn Hoddle would do that all the time, but not me, so why did I do it? Must have been pure instinct.'

Less than two days after the semi-final, however, Liverpool clinched their fourth Championship of Bob Paisley's reign by beating Aston Villa 4–1 at Anfield. As I remember, the occasion was noticeable for a superb chipped pass on the by-line by Terry McDermott which found David Johnson for a tap-in, and Avi Cohen, our left-back, scoring a goal for both teams. When he cancelled out his own-goal by stubbing a shot into the Villa net, the Israeli international celebrated, but it was the Kop chanting 'There's Only One Avi Cohen' which struck a truly bizarre note of internationalism.

Terry McDermott had upped his scoring rate to 11 goals that season by taking most of the penalties, and had produced some wonderful passes for colleagues, as well as going off on those runs for which apparently he didn't have a reason. He was justifiably voted Footballer of the Year in 1980, both by the football writers and his fellow professionals.

Sadly, but I suppose not unexpectedly given Terry's rather self-deprecating style, he didn't get to the ceremony itself where Bob Paisley was waiting to present him with his award. 'It just wasn't me. I didn't enjoy them type of things. And I still don't enjoy them now. Very rarely go to one. I'm a pie-and-peas bloke. Dicky-bows and speeches do nothing for me. I was gonna go, I forced myself to go, but when I got to the train station, there was a delay of an hour, so that was my excuse. I jumped back in the car and went to Chester races instead. Bob Paisley accepted the award on my behalf, and said in his speech, "If Terry's gone on one of his blind-side runs, it'll be his last".'

No offence was taken and Terry resumed with even greater self-confidence on the field for the next season. He was now scoring on a regular basis, and not just from the penalty-spot, as he hit the peak of his form. He scored 13 league goals, but with Liverpool's attention centred on both the European Cup and the League Cup, they caught the eye less than his other contributions. In the League Cup, a trophy for which Liverpool had shown little regard for most of its existence, the team were beginning to hunt it down as an early-season kill, a success from which the momentum could be generated for the remaining major trophies. Liverpool had lost the final to Forest in a replay in 1978, and then been knocked out in the semi-finals in 1980. It was time to get serious.

A relatively benign draw had enabled them to get past Bradford City, Swindon Town, Portsmouth and Birmingham City with ease and then beat Manchester City 2–1 on aggregate in the semi-final. We drew with West Ham at Wembley, but only by virtue of a goal from full-back Alan Kennedy two minutes from the end of extra-time. In the replay at Villa Park, McDermott fashioned a superb chipped pass which Kenny Dalglish crashed home on the volley as the ball dropped over his shoulder for our first goal. Alan Hansen got the second, and Liverpool had their name on the trophy for the first time.

In Europe, McDermott was unstoppable. He rattled home four of the 11 goals which Liverpool put past Oulu Palloseura, the Finnish champions, and then scored an absolute cracker in the first leg of the second round away at Aberdeen (then managed by Alex Ferguson), chipping the ball on the run over the goalie's head from an acute angle on the left of the Aberdeen box.

'The chip? Oh, yeah, I remember that goal. It was a fabulous goal, not because I scored it but because of the build-up, which was just one-touch football played at pace. But, like the others, I don't know what made me try it, chipping with my left foot from that angle. I scored quite a few goals with my left foot, but I wouldn't normally have tried it.'

Terry got another goal, his sixth of the tournament, in the quarter-final first leg at home to CSKA Sofia of Bulgaria, but he can't remember that one, possibly because Graeme Souness took all the attention by hitting a thunderous hat-trick. The semi-final, against Bayern Munich, was a war of attrition, with Liverpool taking a goalless draw to Munich and trying to defend it with a patched-up back four, which included Colin Irwin and Richard Money. That was the night Howard Gayle came on for the injured Dalglish, and proceeded to turn Bayern into nervous wrecks by running at them with pace. Ray Kennedy nicked a goal late on, and though the Germans equalised through Karl-Heinz Rummenigge, they were out of time and Liverpool went into the final by virtue of their away goal.

Apart from one of his runs from the halfway line, after an exchange of passes with Dalglish, Terry McDermott can't recall much about his contribution to the 1981 European Cup final against Real Madrid in Paris. He remembers his fellow ex-Magpie Alan Kennedy scoring, but that was it, such was the anticlimax of the game, with Real Madrid, one of the great names in football, almost scared to attack Liverpool. Only poor Laurie Cunningham, once of Orient and West Brom, and soon to die in a car crash in Spain, showed any attacking flair. But Liverpool had the bottle to win it, and claim their third European crown. Terry, along with Ray Clemence, Ray Kennedy, Phil Neal and substitute Jimmy Case were the only players to have featured in all three wins, a fair measure of how even successful Liverpool sides changed in a relatively short period of time.

The 1981–82 season was to be Terry's last full term at Anfield. There were new players queueing up for places in the first team – Mark Lawrenson had been signed from Brighton as an expert utility player, the untried youngsters Ian Rush and Ronnie Whelan were already making appearances as substitutes, and Sammy Lee and Craig Johnston would soon be pressing for midfield places. A young talent called Kevin Sheedy would have to go elsewhere to make his name. We also had Bruce Grobbelaar as our new goalkeeper.

With a character like Grobbelaar it was always going to be an adventure, and the first part of the season was fairly chaotic, as the goalkeeper and his defence tried to get to know one another. By the time they lost 3–1 at home to Manchester City on a miserable Boxing Day, Liverpool had won only six of their 17 games and were languishing well down the division. Terry McDermott was flying, though, having scored seven goals already, and as the year turned, with Graeme Souness taking over the captaincy, Liverpool produced one of their most famous charges, losing only two of their remaining 25 matches to take the Championship with 87 points, on the new three-points-for-a-win system. Ian Rush was one of the principal catalysts for this, scoring 17 goals in 32 games, but McDermott ended with his highest total ever, 14 for the season.

But he'd also scored three *en route* to another League Cup final, including a penalty on our birthday to beat off Arsenal 3–0 in a fourth-round replay. But it was the youngsters, Whelan and Rush, who won the final for us against Spurs and Ray Clemence.

I got beaten up by Spurs fans outside Wembley afterwards – kicked in the balls, glasses broken – fairly routine stuff compared to the later 'crews', but it meant me driving north that night with my trousers off and a bag of frozen peas packed around my gonads so that I could stand upright at my god-daughter's christening the next day.

For Terry, it was nearly the end. The younger legs coming into the side had begun to out-strip his as Paisley unveiled one of the fastest sides in his managership. A League and League Cup double was no mean way of bowing out. He made just two appearances, as substitute, early the next season before returning to Newcastle, his second home, in September 1982, leaving him to reflect on the success he didn't expect at Anfield.

'Any of those teams between 1976 and 1982 could have won a treble. There were so many good players who had so much confidence in their own ability, and they had the right people to run the club. That's what made the difference between us and the rest.'

Terry's confidence in his own ability may have been a longer time coming, but he was probably a better player for that experience, and is almost certainly a better coach for it, as he now helps Kenny Dalglish build on what Kevin Keegan left at Newcastle. Although he professes that 'Management isn't for me, I'm not the type, going to functions and carrying the burden, I'm not a big name they can look up to,' he retains at least one vital asset upon which Dalglish can rely. For when a player is struggling, or not in form, or looks to have been a bad buy, Terry McDermott will be on hand to say that maybe it's not quite the end of the story.

ALAN HANSEN

Jock One

Those who only know Alan Hansen as the suave, highly articulate critic on *Match of the Day*, as the scourge of 'rank, bad defending', and as the man who donated the phrase 'launch it' to football's vocabulary, will be amused to learn that it was not always thus. For those who *do* know about Hansen's career, especially the early part of it, his transformation into an advocate of safety-first pragmatic defending is a stage device, an act of disguise for the benefit of the television viewers, because we all know that in his heart of hearts, Hansen was, and is, a cavalier rather than a roundhead.

Unquestionably one of the most elegant and creative defenders in European football during his time, Hansen redefined what the likes of Franz Beckenbauer, Uli Stielike and Gaetano Scirea had done for their clubs and countries during the 1970s and '80s. Putting a ball player into the defence gave teams the option of retaining control once a tackle had been won, rather than submitting to the lottery of the long clearance. It also provided new skills, not necessarily tackling, but the ability to read the play and to win the ball by way of interception. Hansen provided all this, with an additional dimension – he attacked, he brought the ball out, he passed, and he set up goals for others and sometimes himself.

Perched in the executive suite of the west London hotel he uses when appearing on *MoTD*, as it is now styled, Hansen remains a picture of relaxed elegance, dressed all in black, seven years on from his retirement from the game. He still looks young enough to play, but a wry smile says otherwise – 'Cannae run five yards now, because I hate it.' He confesses to a nostalgia for training, not for the benefit of fitness but 'for the laughs and the camaraderie', but he also stresses he has no regrets about not playing any more. And who could blame him?

As the only Liverpool player who lasted right through the 1980s, Hansen is a witness to the club's greatest ever haul of trophies, and to a consistency of performance which is unlikely to be matched, even in the cash-rich Premiership. 'In the 13 full seasons I was at Liverpool, we finished Champions eight times, we were runners-up four times, and in 1980–81 we were fifth. That's before you throw in the European Cups (three wins), FA Cups (two) and League Cups (four). I mean, that's frightening.'

In fact, Liverpool's record looks even better if you go back a little, to 1972–73, for from this season to Hansen's last in 1990–91, that fifth place represents the only time Liverpool finished outside the top two in the league during 19 consecutive seasons. The Roman Empire seems a mere blip in history by comparison.

But let's concentrate on 'Big Al' or 'Jocky' as Hansen was called at various times by his team-mates at Liverpool. The astute reader may have discerned a pattern by now – that the players I've chosen are listed not in 'Dream Team' formation, but in a chronological order based not on their débuts but on when they joined the club. So Hansen appears here, ahead of Kenny Dalglish, because Liverpool signed him three months beforehand, almost as a small footnote to the historic 1976–77 season, for £100,000 from Partick Thistle.

'Bob Paisley had never seen me play. The scouts had a look at me, obviously, but Liverpool had this thing that they signed a player on 5 May because their tax year ended on 6 May, and rather than pay tax on the money they had, they'd go and sign somebody, not a big name, just one they'd take a chance on. After me, they signed Frank McGarvey one year, Avi Cohen the next. That was the type of signing I was. [McGarvey didn't play a single first-team game, and Cohen managed only 20 in two seasons.] It was unusual being signed when you hadn't been seen by the manager, but that was the way Liverpool did it with me.'

Hansen was happy to come to Liverpool anyway as he was tiring of Bertie Auld, the Partick manager, who reigned by intimidation, and Partick were certainly happy with the cheque for, as Hansen remembers, 'The club chairman Scot Symon kept getting it out of his pocket to look at it on the train home.' Hansen, then aged 21, had signed without ceremony and gone home, having been instructed to come back to the club in two weeks.

'It was a pretty daunting place to come to, because they were on the verge of winning the title, and were in both the FA Cup and European Cup finals. And here I was coming from Scotland for a relatively small fee. I was wondering what was going to happen because I was going into the first-team dressing-room without knowing any of the other players. It was a big thing for me. I'd been at Partick for four years, and while they were fine to play for, they didn't exactly have the size or stature of Liverpool. But as soon as I went into that dressing-room, the people in there were terrific, they made me feel at home. I watched a reserve game, then played in one, and then they took me to watch the Cup final against Manchester United, and that was it until pre-season training. While the team went off to Rome, I went back to Scotland for the summer.'

By now, Liverpool had developed a basic, but nevertheless distinct, ball-playing central defence with Phil Thompson on the right side and Emlyn Hughes on the left. Both were competitive players and there was no longer a 'big stopper' once Larry Lloyd had moved on in 1974. Both were good tacklers, too, though, and Thompson was pretty good in the air despite his skinny frame. With Tommy Smith near to the veteran stage and Alec Lindsay all but gone, defensive cover was required, which was exactly why the young Hansen was bought. But neither he, nor perhaps even Liverpool, would have expected a début in just the seventh game of the season, with both Thompson and Hughes out injured. It was Saturday, 24 September 1977, a home game against Derby County, and Hansen remembers both it and his subsequent games vividly.

'There must been nearly 50,000 in the ground, and another 10,000 outside. I was scared stiff. I never got a touch of the ball in the first ten minutes. But once I got it and played it a few times, I was all right. To play in front of a crowd like that was a bit special. We won 1–0 with a Terry Mac goal late on. But the next Saturday I had a complete nightmare against Manchester United at Old

Trafford, losing 2–0. We drew 0–0 at Arsenal, beat Leeds and Chelsea and then there was my first derby against Everton. The atmosphere was fantastic. I can remember going out onto the pitch and not being able to hear what I was thinking, the noise was so loud. But it finished 0–0. There were two successive defeats – at home to Villa, away at QPR – but I played in both legs of the first-round European Cup game against Dynamo Dresden [Hansen scored the first goal in the 5–1 home win] but then I got injured. And when they brought me back for another four or five games, I played badly. There were a few defeats [at home to Birmingham City, away at Coventry]. My confidence had gone, the team were going through a bad patch, and I was struggling. They left me out for a long time after that. Even when I went back into the reserves I was having a nightmare. Then, for one reason or another, I just got it back over a period of time, but I couldn't get picked because the team was going so well. Unfortunately for Tommy Smith, he got injured right towards the end of the season, and I had three league games and then found myself in a European Cup final.'

The sight of Hansen warming up on the Wembley turf while Tommy Smith walked the perimeter on his crutches alarmed many fans as they arrived. Hansen was still largely an unknown quantity because he'd been in and out of the team. But that night, and it was a big one despite the negativity which Bruges displayed, Hansen was the epitome of coolness, winning the ball, playing simple passes, reading the game around him and confirming the promise of his partnership with Phil Thompson. 'It was like telepathy with Phil; we had an instant understanding,' Hansen recalls. But if he looked calm on the outside that May night at Wembley, Hansen was all too aware of the momentousness of the occasion.

'The four years beforehand I'd been watching European Cup finals on the telly, sitting with a six-pack and a few mates, and suddenly I was out there. I could hardly believe it. I can remember arriving at Wembley on the coach and thinking, "Well, this is something different." And then when we won it, I just wanted to win it again, to recapture that feeling. Which was exactly the Liverpool mentality – to get success and then want more of it. You remember the emotions, even if you've got a sore head the next morning, and you want the buzz again.'

Liverpool's winning goal was, as we have noted, an all-Scottish number, with Souness and Dalglish combining to complete what must have seemed to Bob Paisley like a very well-judged year's dip into the transfer market – Hansen in May '77, Dalglish in August '77 and Souness in January '78. And this Scottish trio, 'The Three Jocks' as they called themselves, would be at the very heart of Liverpool's achievements over the coming seasons, with Hansen quickly gaining the sort of respect that Dalglish and Souness earned as of right from their Liverpool team-mates.

Ray Clemence, Liverpool's goalkeeper in the first three European Cup finals, remembers the impression Hansen made on him during that first season at the club: 'In the early days, I'd be screaming at him not to take the chances that he took, because I was anticipating that the ball would get robbed off him and then the opposition would be straight through on me. But I came to accept that he was so comfortable on the ball, he was always in control of the situation. Defensively, I could always give him the ball in any situation and know that he'd start something up from it. It's an old saying, but he really was ahead of his time.'

Despite his precociousness, Hansen found himself out of the first team for all but one of the first seven games of the next season, as Alan Kennedy arrived from Newcastle to take up the left-back position, allowing Emlyn Hughes to move back into the centre of defence. But, as Hughes faltered, Hansen was soon claiming the number 6 shirt as his own. 'After that, I never got dropped in 13 years, so I must have been doing something right,' he says.

Hansen played in 34 games of the record-breaking 1978–79 season, scoring his first league goal in a 1–0 win at Wolves in March. More importantly, the back four of Neal, Thompson, Hansen and Kennedy conceded only 16 goals in the season, allowing the midfield and attack to run riot with 85 goals. Hansen has no doubts about the validity of that year's form.

'That was the best Liverpool team I ever played in. It was almost frightening. We were an attacking team who could defend, and though we only won the League that year, the level of performance was phenomenal. I don't think those figures, 85 goals for, 16 against, will ever be bettered, to be honest. I know later teams won the League and the League Cup in the same season, and that we did a treble in 1983–84, but none of those teams was as good as 1978–79. And the team of the late '80s, for all its flair and entertainment, wouldn't have lived with us. That 1978–79 team set the standard by which all Liverpool teams should be judged.'

Hansen is in a unique position to assess this sort of debate – which can keep Liverpool fans talking for hours on end, especially as we haven't won the Championship since 1990 – because he was the only player at the club to last right through the 1980s. Dalglish was there too, of course, but his playing commitments were reduced drastically once he took over as manager in 1985 when Hansen became captain. By then Graeme Souness had moved on to Sampdoria, and you suspect that Hansen's memories are tinged with favouritism for the 'Three Jocks' era, which coincided with the period when his football was at its most daring and expansive.

'I started off as a midfield player at Partick, and then moved to centre-back, so I think for the first six or seven seasons that I was at Liverpool I was more interested in getting the ball and playing than I was in actually defending. Latterly, when I couldnae get forward as much, I still played, but I was probably a better defender between '85 and '90 when I couldn't run so much. Between '77 and '84, running as much as I did, I was all over the place, up and down. I was the centre-back making runs through the inside-right and inside-left positions. It was . . . it was fun!'

For most Liverpool fans, there was one defining Hansen moment, during the match at Everton on 6 November 1982, which we won 5–0, with Ian Rush scoring four goals. With just 11 minutes on the clock, and Everton attacking in their usual frenzied style, Hansen suddenly steps up and stretches to intercept Andy King's intended pass to David Johnson, and immediately moves on at pace, turning outside Steve McMahon's lunging challenge and then accelerating over the halfway line before angling a 40-yard pass behind the retreating Everton defenders right into the stride of Rush on the left, who doesn't even need a touch, so perfect is the pass, allowing him to just sweep it past Southall for an electrifying goal.

Hansen, dribbling the ball to within 15 yards of the Everton penalty area, also passed to Rush to set up the second goal, and as Rush scored his fourth from a run and pass by Sammy Lee, Hansen was making a run alongside him, almost as if he were an auxiliary centre-forward. In a 1980 match at home to Norwich, Hansen appeared more or less on the left wing before cutting inside and thumping a 25-yard right-footer into the top corner. Remember all this the next time he points a finger on *MoTD* at defenders playing around too much!

Perhaps it was the security, not to mention inherent telepathy, of having two Scottish pals up ahead of him which encouraged Hansen to be so bold, but English domestic football has probably never seen another player like him in this mode, and almost certainly never will again. 'The one thing I think Alan fell down on was scoring goals – for a player of his ability, I think he should have scored more,' Ray Clemence says with the hint of a smile – a goalkeeper criticising his centre-half for not getting enough goals!

That this adventurous play was Hansen's own doing, rather than some diktat from the management, the Scot makes quite clear: 'In all my time at Liverpool I was never coached, and I never saw anyone else being coached either. You either adapted to the way Liverpool played or you didn't. Nobody ever sat us down and said, "This is what you do." It was just five-a-side football in training, pass and move, with the occasional discipline of one touch or two. Training was designed basically for people to enjoy themselves, although nobody ever forgot that it was also meant to be hard work. In all my time, we only ever worked on one set-piece – a free-kick routine where one of the full-backs arrived late at the far post, by which Jim Beglin scored against Panathinaikos in 1985. As for corners, we were useless. As soon as we'd won one, we might as well have given the ball back to the opposition because so little came from them. On Friday mornings we'd have a team meeting where no tactics were discussed, just the shape of our team and what the opposition line-up might be. But one of the best "secrets" we carried from the training pitch was that you knew you had a squad of 16 or so guys who you could rely on. That was the difference between us and the others. You didn't necessarily all have to like each other – we did in the main – but you knew that we were all pulling together. There were never any superstars in the dressing-room. If you weren't playing, you picked up the dirty gear off the floor, you just did it by instinct, whoever you were. And on the field the message was that football was not a complicated game, you just kept it simple and enjoyed it.'

Hansen's cavalier period embraced some of the club's greatest successes – a hat-trick of League titles in 1982, '83 and '84, the European Cup wins of '78, '81 and '84 and the four League Cups in a row from '81to '84. While admitting that the European Cup finals were generally 'poor games', Hansen is in no doubt that the 1984 win was 'one of our greatest achievements'. Getting past the champions of Spain (Athletic Bilbao), Portugal (Benfica) and Romania (Dinamo Bucharest) before defeating the Italian champions Roma in their own stadium was fantastic stuff, and Hansen is quick to pay tribute to Joe Fagan, the manager of the time. 'He was a great man; winning a treble in his first year of management was a wonderful achievement, and I don't think he was ever given proper credit for it.'

Hansen reckons that 'Dinamo Bucharest were the best team in the tournament that year', so in defeating them home and away in the semi-final Liverpool had already gone three-parts of the way to winning the trophy. There had been some violence in the first leg – which Graeme Souness describes in his chapter – so the away leg took place in a fevered atmosphere. Souness, booed the moment he appeared, remembers a typical Hansen wind-up during the preliminaries: 'I was down as the villain as far as the Bucharest crowd were concerned so I got a hell of a reception when I got out on the pitch. Of course, as soon as Hansen cottons on to this he's firing all of the six practice balls at me in the kick-about, knowing that I'll get booed every time I get a touch! So there's a bloody great crescendo of jeers cascading down, all for me. But I loved it. Only made me more determined to win.'

Souness remembers that before the final in Rome, Hansen

assumed the role of story-teller, keeping the players laughing and relaxed, to the extent that 'Joe Fagan came in to the dressing-room about 25 minutes before kick-off and had to remind us we had a game to play!'.

What followed in the tunnel as Liverpool prepared to go out for the game in a way foreshadowed what Wimbledon did in the tunnel at Wembley in the 1988 FA Cup final, albeit benignly; the players began to sing the Chris Rea song 'Don't Know What It Is, But I Like It', with the Roma players becoming increasingly unnerved by their opponents' sangfroid. This spilled over into the match as Roma played with rigid caution, even after Phil Neal had poked Liverpool ahead after 14 minutes.

Hansen recalls Roma's terrified approach to the game: 'As soon as it went to 1–1, you could tell there would be extra-time. Roma never went after us in the slightest. We'd never have been allowed to play like that in front of an Anfield crowd. That's probably the difference between English and Italian football, in that we always wanted to win, but our fans would have expected to see something as well. Roma were only concerned with one thing: not losing. The irony was that I was scared of them – I didn't think we had a chance of winning the European Cup in their stadium. Two hours before kick-off, we could see on the telly that the stadium was already half-full of Italians waving flags. So beating Roma on their own patch ranks as one of the great nights.'

The Rome final marked the last game before Graeme Souness left for Sampdoria. Another period of reconstruction began – Mark Lawrenson ('a tremendous utility player', according to Hansen), Ronnie Whelan and Ian Rush were all established, but now the likes of Steve Nicol, John Wark and Kevin MacDonald were in the squad, together with striker Paul Walsh and Irish full-back Jim Beglin. The man with the biggest task, though, was Danish international Jan Molby, trying to replicate the passing skills of Souness, while Steve McMahon was signed to retain the same edge in midfield.

In the circumstances, it was hardly surprising that the 1984–85 season should prove to be a bizarre and traumatic year, as Liverpool were almost as close as 1977 to winning the ultimate treble, but ended instead with no trophies and only the nightmare of Heysel hanging over them. They finished second, 13 points adrift of Howard Kendall's resurgent Everton in the League who beat Liverpool both home and away, lost an FA Cup semi-final replay to Manchester United and, not that it mattered really, went down 1–0 to Juventus in the European Cup final in Brussels.

I have deliberately not pressed any of the players involved on Heysel or indeed Hillsborough. This isn't an attempt to whitewash the club, or to try and rewrite Liverpool's history, but simply to spare the players from going through questions they have been asked a hundred times before, in more meaningful circumstances than a book such as this. The effects on both club and supporters have been well documented, and in the case of Hillsborough are now being investigated by another, long overdue public enquiry. Purely in football terms, the aftermath of Heysel and UEFA's under-standable ban on the club from Europe, provided a sad departure for Joe Fagan, whose resignation had been anticipated; a blight on the careers of many Liverpool players for whom European competition was the ultimate stage on which to perform; and a challenge of morale for the new player-manager Kenny Dalglish and his captain Alan Hansen.

'I didnae want the job, because I thought it was going to be unbelievably difficult being captain with Kenny as a manager while I was his best friend. Fortunately, although the two roles always mean a "them and us" situation, we managed it very well. It helped that I was playing very well at the time, so no difficulties arose on that score. I also became a link between the players and the manager, but the players knew that they could come to me, or that Kenny could come to me with anything, and that I would always take the players' side, unless it was obvious that a player had a less than 100 per cent case. So nothing changed in the relationship, or in the dressing-room, really. I wasn't one of those captains who would rally people if we were 4–0 down, because in those circumstances I was always wanting to go home. But what I was good at was being decent in the dressing-room. I'd give everybody a hard time in a nice way. Used to try and have a laugh, keep the dressing-room on an even keel. I was half-sensible because I knew the way things had been done in the past, so no grievances got out of hand. The squad discipline was good too, so even though we all liked a drink, everybody made sure they were right for a game. There were never any real problems.'

Liverpool clinched the Championship that season with one of their typical power surges, winning 11 of their last 12 league games and drawing the other. Also typical was the way Dalglish came back to score the winning goal at Chelsea, to take the league by just two points from Everton, just a week before the first, historic FA Cup final against them. Molby, it should be recorded in the light of his later indiscretions involving fast cars and alcohol, had an excellent season, with ten goals from 39 games, and he probably swung the Cup final Liverpool's way with his second-half performance after Gary Lineker had out-sprinted Hansen to put Everton ahead in the first half. 'My worst game of the season,' Hansen admits bluntly. 'I'd never played in a Cup final before, and it's different to any other game. I don't know whether it's the long build-up, the press attention or the fact that it's usually a sapping hot day. I went on that pitch that day and thought I was in trouble even in the warm-up!'

But Bruce Grobbelaar's brilliant save of Graeme Sharpe's looping header turned the game, and with Molby now rampant, Ian Rush scored two and Craig Johnston another to complete Liverpool's first Double.

'It was a great high going up to collect the trophy, but the game passed me by so quickly, and it takes ages to come down. I mean, you go for the celebration dinner, and the adrenalin is still pumping. It was a fantastic achievement for Kenny in his first season as manager. Ironically, after 1984–85 and Heysel, I didn't think we were going to be anywhere good enough the following year. And when we were beaten by Everton at home on 22 February 1986, I went out to dinner with Kenny and told him this was the worst Liverpool side I'd ever played in. Then we went on to win the Double, so that was another good tip on my part!'

The 1986–87 season proved to be something of an anticlimax as

Liverpool, having agreed to sell Ian Rush to Juventus in the summer of '87, finished nine points behind champions Everton, and went crashing out of the FA Cup in a second replay at Luton. To cap it all, they lost to Arsenal in the League Cup final, the first time they had been beaten in a game in which Rush had scored. But the purchases of John Aldridge, Peter Beardsley and especially John Barnes created another great Liverpool team (the last?), who won the league by nine points from Manchester United, but who fell to Lawrie Sanchez's goal (and Aldridge's penalty miss) in the Cup final against Wimbledon. Nevertheless, some of the football that season had been truly spectacular, as Hansen remembers with a captain's pride.

'To go 29 games undefeated from the start of the season was special, and the standard of football was terrific. I think with Barnes and Beardsley in the team, with Aldridge a great goalscorer, the entertainment value was enormous. To score 87 goals in 40 games, losing just two matches, was frightening. Barnes and Beardsley were just out-and-out entertainers. Barnes was brilliant that season, and Peter could send three players and 15,000 in the crowd the wrong way with one of his shuffles. It was a great team to play in. If we'd been in the European Cup then, I think we'd have won it.'

Having just missed another Double that season, Hansen went even closer in the next, although everything was utterly over-shadowed by the Hillsborough disaster.

Speaking as someone who thought he'd lost his brother at Sheffield – he had a Leppings Lane ticket but swapped with a friend before the game, and then couldn't get to a phone until seven o'clock that night – I can remember wanting the Liverpool team to withdraw from all further matches that season, so profound was the sense of loss. I'd been to the semi-final the previous season at Hillsborough, also against Forest, and so the experience that fellow fans had suffered that April day was particularly vivid. I could also recall, after 27 years of standing on terraces, how close I and many other fans had been to fatal crushes – at Anfield against Ajax in 1967, and at some of Liverpool's games at Highbury where the Clock End emptied its visiting supporters out through a dark, narrow, suffocating passage. So though I'm middle-aged and designated as middle-class now, I have little nostalgia for the terraces. Football fans deserve the best, after decades of negligence.

Professionally speaking, I found it really hard to sit down and write the last two episodes of the second series of Channel 4's *The Manageress* with such a shadow hanging over the game. But the great majority of the fans, after they'd turned Anfield into a shrine with their scarves and their flowers, urged the team to resume play, which they did heroically in the circumstances, ending with another FA Cup final victory over Everton, and that never-to-be-forgotten last-second loss of the championship to Arsenal.

When the final whistle of that epic match sounded I remember feeling, for the first time ever, that a Liverpool defeat didn't matter any more. God only knows how the players recovered their love of the game after all the funerals they attended. As we now know, Kenny Dalglish was eventually overwhelmed by the grief and the strain, so it's not a hollow tribute to Alan Hansen that he was able to rally his team-mates the next season to win the club's 13th Championship of the modern era, their 18th in all.

Hansen himself, though was feeling another sort of strain, particularly after the bizarre 4–3 defeat to Crystal Palace in the semi-final of the FA Cup. 'The Palace game was one of those games where you play for 45 minutes and, if it was boxing, the ref would have had to stop it, because Liverpool were so far in front it was untrue. I remember thinking during it, "We cannot get beaten here," because we'd been all over them, yet we were still only one goal up at half-time. I'd played David Burrows in on the left-hand side so many times that he came in at the interval with his tongue hanging out.

'Then the second half was just mad. If there was ever an example where you can't take things too easy at football, that was the one. We relaxed and we couldn't get it back. I didn't think it was the end of an era with that defeat, because although I was 35 by then, I wasn't losing any pace, but maybe my stamina was not so good. The worrying part came after we'd clinched the Championship, during the summer when the mental stress of playing at the top for 14 seasons caught up with me. I was over at my golf club at Hillside, and normally after a round I'd just drink mineral water or something, even in a close season. Suddenly I fancied a pint, and I had two pints of lager; looking back, I think something was trying to tell me "I've had enough of this". Physically, I could have kept going; it was the mental side of things that I was finding tough. I'd been finding I couldn't get to sleep at night during the closing part of the season, working out what results we needed, and when it hits you like that I knew I was in trouble.'

Hansen officially retired early in 1991, about a week after Dalglish had quit the managership as the stress of the past two years finally caught up with him. It seemed somehow symbolic that these two great Scottish players should sever the cord with Liverpool at the same time, so closely had their careers and their friendship been linked. Indeed, there were plenty of rumours that Hansen was sounded out about the Liverpool manager's job, but though he'll neither confirm nor deny these stories, he's emphatic that management was not for him.

'If you're feeling the pressure as a player, what would it have been like as a manager? The expectancy at Liverpool is enormous. The difference lies between us winning the Championship in 1990 and United winning the Premiership in 1993. They were doing a lap of honour for six months afterwards, while for us in 1990 it was "So what? Just another championship, wasn't it?" That's expectancy, that's pressure, even when you're winning; so what would it be like when you're losing? I spoke to a former Liverpool guy who went to a top-six club and I asked him what it was like after three months and he smiled and said. "No pressure, magic." That's the difference.'

So now Hansen is able to watch football, both on professional duty for *MoTD* and privately, and still enjoy it without missing playing one bit. He's also an adviser to a recently created Football Investment Trust, which reflects the game's new profile as a source of great interest for the City. Had this been happening a decade or so ago Hansen would probably have been rated as a blue-chip investment all by himself. His column in the *Radio Times* and his laconic send-up, in the advert for Littlewoods, of his 'dour critic' persona, almost certainly earn him more money now than he ever did playing, but he has no doubt about the true value of his time at Liverpool: 'It was a great place to be – top-class players and top-class people running the club, and a wonderful atmosphere in the dressing-room. I don't think we had one year where there was any trouble in there.'

Thanks to Alan Hansen's unique style of play, Liverpool didn't have much trouble on the pitch either. 'He was the best footballing centre-half, bar none,' Graeme Souness says, 'just so clever and cute, and with so much pace he could kill people with the ball at his feet.'

KENNY DALGLISH

Jock Two

'He was the best,' Graeme Souness says with emphasis, 'just the best'. No Liverpool supporter would argue with Graeme's assessment of his fellow Scot Kenny Dalglish – few would dare argue with Souness about anything – but coming from a man who is passionately dedicated to football and achievement through it, speaking about a man with an equivalent if not greater drive, it carries more weight than if it was anyone else who asserted it, no matter how sincere their judgement. Whatever Liverpool fans may think of him after his unfortunate spell as manager of the club from 1991–94, Souness loves his football and, as the novelist Howard Jacobson might opine, 'he knows whereof he speaks'.

'Kenny was the best I ever played with, the best British footballer I saw in my time in the game. The only player I've seen who was better, whom I played against in a fairly meaningful charity game in Italy, was the Brazilian Zico. So that's where Kenny is in the scale of things. And above and beyond his ability, he had a quality that all great players must have – he was completely fearless. I remember when he got injured in a home match against Manchester United [on 2 January 1984] . The ball had been fired in, and Kenny went for it but ended up heading Kevin Moran's elbow or his wrist where he was wearing a brace, and he went down in a heap. I was the first one to him, and he was already saying, "I'm all right, I'm all right." But the moment he took his hands off his face you could see that his whole bloody cheek had just collapsed. And yet the bugger wanted to play on! He staggered to his feet and was ready to play on. Of course, he had to go off and go straight to hospital, but we had to more or less drag him off the pitch. He ended up having a metre of packing in his cheek to build it up again, and he was out for a couple of months. He had the heart of a lion.'

When Kenny Dalglish joined Liverpool from Celtic in August 1977, for what now seems like the bargain of the century of £440,000 (although it was a British record at the time), Liverpool were already champions of Europe and champions of England. It was assumed, because he quickly donned the number 7 shirt, that Kenny was a direct replacement for Kevin Keegan, but Bob Paisley told me later that year that he wished he 'could have had both of them in the same team'. In other words, it was not a case of like-for-like. Kenny was a completely different player from Keegan, not in terms of heart and attitude, but in the way he played and the way he linked up with the players around him. While Keegan was an all-action buzzer, who made his pace and his non-stop running his chief assets, Kenny was a player of infinite guile and strength. It was with Dalglish in mind that Paisley uttered his now famous dictum on football 'that the first five yards is all in the head'. With Dalglish it seemed more like ten yards, such was his speed of thought, his ability to see the play around him and what opportunities it presented. He was also, it goes without saying, a fantastic striker from any range. He got goals from five yards and 25 yards.

Apart from television clips, I'd first seen him in the flesh playing for Scotland in a vital World Cup qualifying game against Czechoslovakia at Hampden Park in September 1973. My pal Richard White and I had interrupted our tour of western Scottish pubs when we learned of the match, and headed into Glasgow where we were able to buy a couple of tickets, at face value, from a guy outside the ground. They were for the Celtic end of the stadium, and Richard and I tried to disguise our Englishness by buying tammies and tartan scarves before the game. Just as well, because England were also playing that night – a friendly against Austria which they won 7–0 – and every time an England goal was reported on the supporters' radios, there was booing all around us. Surrounded by mad Jocks, many of whom had the infamous 'brown bags' in their hands, we got by on grunts of approval and cheers as Dalglish, wearing the number 10 jersey, played alongside Denis Law and helped Scotland to a famous 2–1 victory. It didn't matter that Joe Jordan had replaced Dalglish and gone on to score the winning goal, because all around us the Celtic fans were hailing King Kenny's part in the win. He was almost a god as far as they were concerned, so when we signed him I was both aware of his fame and reputation, but also shocked that Celtic had ever agreed to let him go. Their loss was to be our massive gain.

I saw his first game for Liverpool, in the 1977 Charity Shield against Manchester United at Wembley. It ended a goalless draw, but there was no doubt that Kenny would do for us, so fluid was his movement, so sharp was his passing. A week later, Dalglish made his league début for us at Middlesbrough and scored inside seven minutes from a pass by Terry McDermott.

Terry, currently Dalglish's assistant at Newcastle United, remembers his first impressions of the new man in the number 7 shirt: 'What struck you first was that his technique was just so perfect. His control, his ability to hold the ball up and shield it from defenders, the way he brought other players into the game with one pass, and his instant reaction to a goalscoring chance. He was a different player to Kevin, but you could tell that he was going to be as great, if not greater.'

Dalglish scored in his next game too, ironically against Newcastle, as the Kop got their first sight of him and roared their approval with a hand-clapping routine and a shout of 'Dal-glish!'. When he scored in his third game, in a 3–0 win over West Brom, the love affair had already begun to blossom into a passion. All the doubts we had about Keegan being irreplaceable vanished within a few games. It was a case of 'The king is dead, long live the king'.

Dalglish played in all 42 league games that first season, scoring 20 goals and making countless others as we finished second, seven points adrift of Forest. He also scored seven in our run to the final of the League Cup, which we also lost to Forest in a replay at Old Trafford. But, most importantly, given our new status in Europe, he helped Liverpool to their second successive European Cup final, scoring in the home wins against Benfica (4–1) and our victims of the previous year Borussia Moenchengladbach (3–0), before getting that famous winner at Wembley against Bruges.

Kenny had apparently noticed from two earlier shots by Terry McDermott that the Belgian goalkeeper Jensen had a habit of going down early rather than staying on his feet till the last moment. So when Graeme Souness played what seemed like an exquisite volleyed pass into Dalglish's path – and Souness has the real version of this in the next chapter – Kenny simply waited for the keeper to flatten himself before chipping the ball over his prostrate body into the far corner of the net. From up where I was sitting, it looked almost as though Dalglish had mis-hit the ball, so slowly did it travel, but when we saw it nestling in the onion bag, bedlam ensued all around us. Even so, our gang noticed, and went on to appreciate every time he did it, that Dalglish ran not to his team-mates in self-congratulation, but to the fans, hurdling the advertising hoardings, almost as if he wanted to be in there with them celebrating. It seemed then, and was proved over the many years and goals that followed, that Dalglish was as one with the supporters. Our joy was his. And 30 goals in his first season brought an awful lot of joy.

Forest did us again early the next season, knocking us out of the European Cup, and, with an early exit from the League Cup at Sheffield United – not a trophy we thought much of at that stage – it looked like a straightforward task for Liverpool that season: Cup and League. God, we were so demanding by then. Dalglish duly repeated his feat of the first season by scoring the first goal in a 2–1 home win over QPR. The famous 7–0 win over Spurs followed on 2 September, and though everyone remembers Terry Mac's goal, it should be pointed out that Kenny scored the first two inside 20 minutes to demoralise the Spurs defence. He went on to score nine goals in the first 11 games to give the Reds an unbeaten start, which set the tone for the whole season.

At this stage of my life, I was living in London, seeing all the 'away' games there, going back to Liverpool for the big matches, and also conducting a commuting romance with a girl from Birmingham who was a mad West Brom supporter – she was also doing a PhD at Birmingham University, so was ahead of her time in terms of the game attracting bright women. The rough agreement was that I'd travel up for the weekends when they were at home, and she'd travel to London or Liverpool when I wanted to see the Reds. On 23 September, we satisfied both our football passions by going to see Liverpool at the Hawthorns. West Brom were a fantastic side to watch in those days, with Cyrille Regis and Laurie Cunningham up front – they'd stuck seven past Coventry early in the season – and a young Bryan Robson in midfield, and they actually became serious challengers to Liverpool for a good part of that season. Cunningham duly sprinted away from the Liverpool defence on the halfway line to slot a shot past Ray Clemence, but with 20 minutes to go Dalglish scored what was probably his cheekiest goal ever.

It had echoes of his goal against Bruges, in that he had obviously been studying the habits of the Baggies' goalkeeper, Tony Godden. Whenever he gathered the ball, Godden would wait for the forwards and his defence to move back upfield before dropping the ball to his feet.

As one Liverpool attack petered out, Dalglish hung back over the by-line and watched as Godden began to dribble the ball out. In a flash, he pounced, stealing the ball off the hapless keeper and tucking it into the back of the net. For several seasons afterwards, and even to this day, you will see goalkeepers conspicuously look behind them as their penalty area clears to check that there isn't a forward lurking, such was the impact of Dalglish's goal on their profession. The one George Best 'scored' for Northern Ireland, when he toed the ball free as Gordon Banks threw it up for his kick has nothing on Kenny's. I know I'm biased, but then Kenny's goal is in the record-book and Best's isn't. So there.

By the time of the return match against West Brom at Anfield on 3 February 1979, they were actually at the top of the First Division, one point ahead of Liverpool, thanks to their own exuberant play and a few postponements for us in January. 'West Brom are real challengers,' Bob Paisley warned in his programme notes. A crowd of over 52,000 reflected Anfield's anxiety for a result and Kenny duly delivered after 21 minutes. Taking Terry McDermott's squared pass in the box, Dalglish calmly sidefooted the ball past Godden into the bottom right-hand corner. David Fairclough got a second after the interval, to see us home 2–1. I'd introduced my girlfriend to the joys of standing on the Kop that day, but it was a pretty silent weekend after my team had beaten her Baggies.

Dalglish scored one of his classics at the end of that month at Derby County, as he picked up the ball in midfield and turned Derby's six-foot defender Vic Moreland before advancing towards the goal. To his credit, Moreland got back and attempted to tackle Dalglish but was bounced to the turf by a swivel of Kenny's hips before he blasted a left-foot shot home from 20 yards. Moreland weighed 12 stone, but Dalglish flicked him off like a matador dispensing with a bull's lunge. It was a trademark demonstration not only of his shooting power, but also his strength on the ball and his ability to fight off defenders.

Graeme Souness was frequently a close-range witness to such skills: 'It was just something else he had, apart from all the other stuff – the ability to have his weight in the right place at the right time, so that as defenders came in at him, from the side or behind, he was able to just bounce them off because his balance was so perfect. He had such strength in his legs and in his hips.'

Dalglish contributed 21 league goals to Liverpool's total of 85 that season, but it was probably no coincidence that our attacking midfield players – well, they were all attacking come to think of it – scored 33 between them, as they worked the ball into Kenny and took advantage of his flicks and passes into space or to feet. Souness, who scored eight times, thinks he might have had even more had Dalglish let him see more of the ball.

'When you're battling to win the ball in midfield, head down, sometimes all you can see is the socks, so often I'd have to bobble a pass into Kenny, or fire it or volley it, and he would always kill it stone dead. I'd move again, of course, but because he was so good, because he could see so much, I'd make a run and find that he'd already helped the ball out somewhere else. It used to drive me bonkers sometimes, because 99 times out of 100 when I played a ball into a forward and made a run, I'd expect to get it back. But often he'd already seen something nobody else had, and my run would be turned into a decoy. He was just so clever, it was unbelievable.'

It should really have been Liverpool's first Double in 1979 but our FA Cup bogey team, Manchester United, knocked us out in a semi-final replay at Goodison Park after Dalglish and Hansen had scored to earn us a 2–2 draw in the first tie. At the time I think I rationalised United's apparent hold over us in terms of the FA Cup as being something to do with it needing victory in only six matches to win the trophy, which suited the United team of the time rather more than having to put in a whole season's effort. Just a theory, of course. Nevertheless, Dalglish was named Footballer of the Year for the first time, after just two seasons in the English league.

Another Championship the following year was more than fair compensation. Dalglish was an ever-present for the third season running, scoring 'just' 16 goals this time round, but the evidence of his ability to create goals as often as he would score them came with David Johnson's tally of 21, as the ex-Evertonian confirmed his status as Dalglish's regular striking partner.

One Dalglish speciality was to receive the ball from the right wing, almost at the angle of the penalty box, with his back to goal and a defender right up his backside, whereupon he would feint one way and pass another to set up either a cross from the by-line or a shot from the edge of the box. It was just such a move which allowed our Israeli left-back Avi Cohen to make amends for an earlier own-goal, by driving Dalglish's pass home to give Liverpool the lead in the Anfield match against Aston Villa on 3 May 1980, the eventual 4–1 win clinching Dalglish's third trophy in three seasons at Liverpool. A European Cup and two Championships had not been too bad for starters.

It should be mentioned that our 1979–80 European campaign lasted just two games, as our 2–1 lead from the home leg in the first round against Dynamo Tbilisi was wiped out by an emphatic 3–0 win in Georgia. I disgraced myself that night in the eyes of a few cultured friends by bringing my transistor and earpiece into a group outing to the theatre so that I could listen to the game. As the goals crackled into my ear, it became the football equivalent of 'How did you enjoy the play, Mrs Lincoln?'.

Meanwhile, our other FA Cup bogey team, Arsenal, knocked us

out of the competition in the third replay of the semi-final, though we did an effective job of softening them up for West Ham in the final. In the League Cup, Forest completed their third seriously irritating win over us in successive seasons, knocking us out in the semi-final.

In the 1980–81 season, Dalglish suffered a rare spell of fallibility after 180 consecutive appearances by getting injured early on. He missed eight league games in all that season, and registered only eight goals. He wasn't alone – that familiar barometer of Liverpool's duff seasons, the number of players used, indicated both wide-scale injuries and loss of form. Only Phil Neal played his full quota of matches, and no fewer than 23 different players found their way onto the team-sheet.

Everton put us out of the FA Cup in the fourth round, but we finally got our hands on the League Cup, as seven Dalglish goals helped us to meet, then beat, West Ham in a replayed final at Villa Park. His goal there was one of his best – volleying in Terry McDermott's floated pass as it dropped over his right shoulder. It was just as well for Terry that he'd seen Dalglish's run, because 'if you ever missed one, or passed badly, Kenny would give you The Stare afterwards'. Meanwhile, the selection of the youngster Ian Rush, after just one league appearance, for such an important game was, though we didn't know it at the time, a significant moment in the club's history.

Dalglish played in all the European Cup games that year as Liverpool marched towards Paris and their third victory in the tournament. Though he was injured and substituted in the second leg of the semi-final against Bayern Munich, and substituted late on in the final itself, he must have taken great satisfaction from the 5–0 aggregate win over Alex Ferguson's Aberdeen – he scored in the 4–0 home win – and, of course, in yet another European Cup winners' medal.

All I got, apart from the thrill of seeing my third European Cup win by Liverpool, was the equivalent of a loser's medal. My West Brom girlfriend and I had agreed to split up – well, I'd bowed to her decision – before the final, but we decided to go ahead with the trip anyway. The romance of Paris achieved nothing, and after being bummed out of the team hotel, we found ourselves drinking quietly with John Peel and that veteran of Liverpool's pop and humour group The Scaffold, John Gorman, in a bar around the corner. When I say 'with', we were in the same bar, that's all.

Having 'failed' in the league by finishing fifth, Liverpool immediately set out to rectify matters in 1981–82. Mark Lawrenson, Ronnie Whelan and, eventually, Ian Rush were all brought in to add fresh legs, while Craig Johnston also began to emerge as a bustling midfielder-cum-winger. Bruce Grobbelaar was now in goal after Clemence's departure. Dalglish was back to full health too, putting in his more traditional 42 games, and though he was less prolific than usual with 13 league goals, the fact that Rush scored 17 in just 32 appearances, confirmed that a major new striking partnership had been formed.

Rush's pace and ability to harass defenders allowed Kenny to play a slightly deeper role, where he could be both provider and scorer, linking up with the midfield surges of new captain Graeme Souness, who took over from Phil Thompson after a string of poor results in the autumn. These may or may not have been connected with the death on 29 September 1981 of Bill Shankly, the founding father of the modern Liverpool. It certainly affected me, as I reflected on the two occasions I'd met him, first at the car wash in 1971 when he turned up with Cup final tickets, and then later in the 1970s when I attended the launch of his LP record giving a spoken account of his life and times at the London International Press Centre. He was standing alone when I reintroduced myself gawkily as the kid who had once cleaned his car and who had now become a writer and occasional sports journalist with *Time Out* magazine. 'You're doing well for yourself, son,' he said, before adding 'you've even got a suit, I see.'

I got him to autograph my copy of the record, which I still treasure, and wished him all the best, knowing that nothing but being involved with Liverpool again would be the best. Like most exiled Scousers, I made the pilgrimage to Anfield for the first game after his death, against Swansea City on Saturday, 3 October. The

Kop chanted his name incessantly before a cavernous minute's silence. Liverpool, both the team and the city, seemed distracted that day. Terry McDermott's two penalties helped us scrape a draw but there was an overwhelming feeling of sadness. I'm sure Shankly approved of Dalglish. He was a player who perfectly reflected the great man's standards. Brave, skilful, passionate, aware of an obligation to the supporters and, by no means least, seemingly impervious to injury.

Liverpool's declining form hit its lowest point with a 3–1 home defeat by Manchester City on Boxing Day. Going home for Christmas was still routine, but that visit was particularly depressing. Almost miraculously, however, Liverpool hit form in the New Year and rocketed up the table by winning 20 and losing only two of their remaining games. Dalglish and Rush scored 22 of their 30 goals in that period to lift us to another Championship, while their 13 goals – Rush eight, Dalglish five – won us another League Cup, beating Spurs in extra-time in the final after being a goal down.

In the next season they scored 42 goals between them in the league, and everyone cited the first goal in a 3–1 win over Watford as a prime example of the partnership. Dalglish controlled a difficult ball and shrugged off a defender seemingly in one movement, before slicing a pass through the Watford defence that Rush instantly buried with a left-foot drive. In contrast to the previous year's festive season, Liverpool also thumped Manchester City 5–2 with Dalglish scoring a glorious hat-trick. The League Cup was also claimed again, with a sweet victory over Manchester United.

Dalglish had yet another ever-present season, and topped the Championship/League Cup double by winning both the Player of the Year award, made by the Footballer Writers Association, and the PFA award, in an overwhelming endorsement by his peers. Rush won the Young Player award. Dalglish's form had reached a new level of perfection that season, as Alan Hansen recalls: 'If you lay aside his footballing ability, what else shone through was his sheer will to win. He would be trying as hard in the 90th minute as in the first, and he never hid. Like all great players, he'd always give you something, whether he was having a quiet game or not. I was still bringing the ball out a lot in those days, and if you look at any of the pictures I'm always gesturing for him to "show" for a pass. But what the photos wouldn't show was Kenny pointing a finger down one side of his shorts or the other to show where he wanted me to play the ball. It worked a treat every time. You could give him the ball in almost any situation and he'd make something of it.'

And Ian Rush, who'd overcome his earlier distaste for Dalglish's withering dressing-room banter, or 'slaughtering' as they called it, had also come to appreciate what the experienced Scot was now doing for him professionally: 'Kenny was fantastic towards me now I was established in the first team. He was always giving me bits of advice on the field during matches, making me more aware of situations and patterns of play, and pointing out weaknesses in the opponents' defence. And it became a case of when I made any sort of run, he'd be able to find me with a pass and play me in on goal.'

The advice bore spectacular fruit in the 1983–84 season, the first under new manager Joe Fagan, as Rush rattled in 32 goals in just 41 league games. And though Dalglish's scoring input was tailing off – he got seven in that injury-disrupted season – at least two of his efforts were classics. On 10 September at Arsenal, Liverpool produced a quite stunning passing move, switching the ball from one side of the pitch to another, as Hansen fed Rush, who passed across field to Sammy Lee and then found Dalglish on the edge of the Arsenal area. Dalglish played in Michael Robinson, a new signing from Brighton, and he produced an inspired back-heel to throw the Arsenal defence. Still way out on the right of the Arsenal area, Dalglish turned inside and curled a sublime left-foot shot up into the far top corner of Arsenal's net.

A similar goal arrived against Ipswich in November, when Kenny took a short corner from Sammy Lee and promptly curled another left-footer over Paul Cooper into the top corner. That goal marked yet another historic achievement for Dalglish, as he became the first player ever to score one hundred goals for one club in Scotland and then complete another century for a club in England.

The dressing-room at the time, as Alan Hansen recalls, was

absolutely buzzing: 'The worst time before a match for me was between 2.15 p.m. and 2.55 p.m., when I was backwards and forwards to the toilet. But one way of settling the nerves was to set up these joke routines, where someone would offer an opinion and then we'd all react. But when the likes of Ronnie Whelan or Rushie would say something, we'd all pretend not to have heard them. It helped keep us all relaxed. And there was terrific atmosphere in there while we were winning. Dalglish was always in the middle of all this. People in the press who say he's introverted have got it all wrong, because he's got a fantastic sense of humour.'

But the atmosphere could soon change after a bad result. One such was a 4–0 defeat at Coventry that season, with Liverpool three goals down by half-time, a performance which prompted Dalglish and Souness into differing views about what was to be done. Souness recalls these disputes with a wide smile: 'Kenny and I would often very nearly come to blows in the dressing-room at half-time because we both felt strongly about something. Bob or Joe would just leave us to it and go off and have a cup of tea while we tried to sort things out, shouting at each other and shoving.'

Alan Hansen was also a witness to these half-time discussions. 'The two of them were just so competitive and opinionated, very strong characters. Mind you, I wasn't too far behind some times. But Kenny and Graeme, even though they were mates, would have ended up arguing over a tiddlywinks match.'

The competitive spirit saw Liverpool sweep to a treble that year – the League for the third year running; the League Cup for the fourth year running; and the European Cup for the fourth time. Graeme Souness and Ian Rush talk in detail later about that European campaign, in which Dalglish scored three goals, and Rush five.

But the following season was an anticlimax, and worse. Liverpool finished second in the league, were knocked out of the FA Cup in the semi-final by Manchester United, finally lost a League Cup tie, to Tottenham, and then there was Heysel.

I didn't go that year, or the one before in Rome. But my brother did. He witnessed some terrible attacks on Liverpool fans in Rome after 1984, and believes that some simmering resentment against the Italians helped fuel that mad charge across the terraces at Heysel. Mind you, he also played football outside the stadium with Italian fans before the match. It was a dreadful night, which made you wonder why you ever supported football let alone Liverpool.

Yet part of the healing process came with the appointment of Kenny as player-manager, who in turn made Alan Hansen his captain. They both conducted themselves magnificently in that post-Heysel season, and though Dalglish played in only 17 games, nine of those were in the run-up to the title, in which Liverpool won 11 and drew one of the their last 12 games. He scored one goal in the 2–1 win at West Brom, and then, with the timing of a true man of destiny, he popped in the winner against Chelsea at Stamford Bridge in the last game – a small matter of controlling a high ball on his chest and then volleying it on the run as it dropped. A week later, the Cup and with it the classic Double was won, as Rush and Molby took Everton apart in the second half at Wembley.

When the match at Chelsea finished, one of the first men out to congratulate Dalglish was Bob Paisley who by now had been elevated to a directorship and the role of adviser to Dalglish. How different would Liverpool's history have been if the club had awarded a similar role to Shankly, I wonder? Paisley and Dalglish hugged each other like father and son on a wedding day – the lineage had been successfully maintained. Shankly to Paisley, Paisley to Fagan, Fagan to Dalglish.

One of the men who suffered at the hands of Liverpool that season was Gary Lineker, whose single season at Everton won him the Footballer of the Year award, but also, thanks to Liverpool, two runners-up places as well. And his view on the man who did a great deal to spoil his season? 'Kenny was one of the all-time great players. One of the best I've ever played against. To play up front with him was a licence to print goals. The way he could let the ball go, but still keep his body between it and his marker was amazing. Not just in the shielding of the ball but also because he could then turn and get a pass in. I played with him once, in a testimonial at Tottenham, I think, and it was exactly the same experience as when I played half a game with Michel Platini. Kenny had a similar sort of awareness and instinct for where to go. He was a fantastic finisher too, a supremely intelligent footballer. He was also a tremendous competitor – he was a right "whinger" on the pitch, because he hated losing anything, even a throw-in!'

Dalglish played very few games after that wonderful Double season, perhaps sensing that it was the right sort of high note on which to end a playing career. But for an encore, as manager, he won the Championship twice more, and the FA Cup again. Hillsborough, by his own admission, placed an enormous and ultimately unbearable strain on him, and he was right to get out, not just for his own health, but for the happiness of his family.

I regret that Liverpool didn't do more to nurse him back – but then it's not always been the club's style to show sensitivity. The fact that Kenny has since stormed back into the game, at Blackburn and now Newcastle, speaks volumes for his resilience, and for what Liverpool have lost.

'Kenny's always had the drive to keep winning,' Souness says of a man who, in a way, is his emotional twin. 'He's just second to none.'

GRAEME SOUNESS

Jock Three

The scariest moment in Alan Bleasdale's Liverpool-based serial *Boys from the Blackstuff* came when champion head-butter Yosser Hughes stumbled into the reception area of a smart nightclub and found Graeme Souness sitting on a sofa with club-mate Sammy Lee. Hughes, played with wild-eyed mania by Bernard Hill, approaches Souness with the classic pest's line, 'You're that Graeme Souness, aren't you?'

For all Liverpool fans there was a wonderful in-joke going on here, as we were invited to expect Yosser to meet his match in tackling our hardest player. For Bleasdale's placement of Souness in the scene was a knowing salute to the man whose fierce tackling and competitive manner had swiftly endeared him to the fans when he arrived at the club in January 1978.

As I remember, the potential confrontation between the fictional hard man and the real thing ended in nothing more than Yosser comparing moustaches with Souness, before he beat a respectful retreat. Out on the football field, too, there was only one winner, as Graeme Souness powered Liverpool to win 12 of the game's major trophies in the six and a half seasons he played for them. 'During the whole period I was there,' Souness confirms, 'we won either the Championship or the European Cup in every season, and then both in my last. It was a nice time to be playing.'

Graeme doesn't frame this last sentence as a smart-arse under-statement. He says it sincerely because, as anyone who watched him play must know, he loved Liverpool, and despite the fact that it nearly cost him his life, and *did* cost him his job when he was the manager, his passion for this club, and for football, still burns.

131

When we talked, over a cup of tea in the canteen at Southampton's training ground on a working morning, with a scouting trip up to London beckoning, he kept extending the time he'd allocated for me because he was simply enjoying himself so much as the memories kept pouring out. He insisted on giving me his phone number in case I wanted to ask further questions, or if I needed clarification about anything he'd said. It crossed my mind that my publishers should really have got Graeme to write this book, because talking about Liverpool is obviously one of his favourite pastimes.

It was no real surprise that when Southampton's new-style board of directors set new limits on previous spending promises at the end of his first season there, Graeme Souness should leave the club. No surprise either that he should go back to Italy, where he'd played for Sampdoria for two seasons in the mid-1980s, to manage Serie B team Torino. He loves the culture and the climate out there, as we shall hear. But nobody should think he's taking an easy option. After managing Glasgow Rangers, Liverpool, Galatasaray in Turkey and Southampton, he's plainly a wealthy man. But, despite this, and his triple bypass operation in 1992, Souness just can't let go, can't stop looking for challenges, can't give up mainlining football, because he just loves it too much.

Now those who don't support Liverpool, and those who do but who turned against him when he was manager there, always try to write him off as being too turbulent, too aggressive in his nature. He put noses out of joint as a manager and, say his critics, bones out of joint when he was playing. Certainly his tackling was of 'a terrible beauty' (Yeats – W.B., not Ron), but his running was dynamic, his passing precise and his shooting thunderous. All this in just one player. I can remember from my first interview with Bob Paisley in February 1978, a few weeks after Souness had signed, that he said, 'Most midfields are made up of a buzzer type of player, a cruncher for winning the ball, and a spreader for the passing. This lad, Souness, is all three.'

Souness, who had joined Spurs as a 17-year-old before moving north to Middlesbrough in December 1972, had already won Scottish international honours at every level when Liverpool became interested in him. 'Phil Boersma had come to Middlesbrough from Liverpool, and was sharing digs with me,' recalls Souness. 'He told me that he'd heard there was some interest in me back at Anfield. I'd been out in Australia on tour in May 1977, and we'd watched Liverpool against Borussia Moenchengladbach on the telly in a hotel in Wollongong. Of course it was full of Germans at the time, but I can remember thinking that Liverpool were *the* team. Eventually an offer came in which Boro turned down. This unsettled me a bit, to say the least, so I pressed John Neal, the manager, for the move and he reluctantly agreed to release me. It didn't end nicely, but seven months on from that night in Australia I was a Liverpool player, and it was a great thrill.'

Souness went straight into the first team for the away game at West Brom, which Liverpool won 1–0, but two defeats, to Birmingham City and Coventry City, followed before Souness impressed himself on the home fans with a great first goal against Manchester United on Saturday, 25 February 1978. Terry McDermott's curling cross from the right was met by a confident swing of Souness's left foot and the volley rocketed past Gary Bailey from 15 yards. Liverpool won the game 3–1, and though their form dipped early in March, they finished with a run of 12 unbeaten games, embracing nine wins, but it wasn't enough to catch Nottingham Forest (who, apart from leaving us in second place, had also knocked Liverpool out in the semi-final of the League Cup). Nevertheless, Souness was as impressed with Liverpool from the inside as he had been from the outside.

'I wouldn't say I was intimidated by coming here, but it was obviously a major step up in class for me,' he recalls. 'The training régime was all about making sure the players were right in the head – there was no coaching as such – and about keeping them motivated. But you just had to look around the dressing-room on match-days. There'd be two internationals on the subs' bench, and another four sitting there with their clothes on, so that was all you needed to keep you on your toes. Everybody was playing for their place; that was the Liverpool way.'

The European Cup beckoned again, as Souness came on in the

away leg of the semi-final against Borussia Moenchengladbach, which was lost 2–1, but David Johnson scored a morale-boosting goal just two minutes from time.

In the home leg, with Jimmy Case, Terry McDermott, Souness and Ray Kennedy bossing the midfield, the Germans were swept away 3–1, with goals from Kennedy, Dalglish and Case. So, like Alan Hansen, Souness found himself in a European Cup final just a year after watching Liverpool's first win in Rome on television. Typically, he made an historic contribution: 'It was a pretty boring game because Bruges never came to play us at all; they were very defensive and just sat back, and we had lots of the ball but couldn't do much with it. But on 65 minutes we got the breakthrough we needed. I know my pass to Kenny looked good on the telly, but the reality was that as the ball was dropping from the sky, I was turning blind into it, and I'm thinking, "I've just got to go solid here because I'm gonna get kicked." And as I went, I think the other guy half-pulled out of the tackle, and I was just conscious of trying to help the ball into space, but it fell nicely for Kenny who took it with his first touch. I got a lot of credit, but it was for something not quite intended. But the feeling afterwards was magnificent. It became a taste that you enjoyed so much. So that when you did come unstuck, which we did on occasions, it really hurt.'

The pain was fairly quick in arriving the next season as Liverpool were instantly deposed by Forest in the first round in September, losing 2–0 at the City Ground to goals by Gary Birtles – at least this helped convince Manchester United to buy him later! – and full-back Colin Barrett. Forest then clung on for a goalless draw at Anfield. 'They were a boring lot, Forest,' Souness says scathingly. 'We had all the ball against them but Peter Shilton stopped us scoring, while Kenny Burns and Larry Lloyd just stood there and headed the ball clear while we attacked and attacked, and they'd try and hit us on the counter.'

Nevertheless, that early upset, coming after a first-round League Cup exit to Sheffield United in August, stiffened Liverpool's resolve for the rest of the season.

Souness, now established in the number 11 shirt, galvanised the midfield around him into both making and scoring goals. 'It was never mentioned,' he recalls of the mood in the dressing-room before games, 'but in 1978–79 it was really a case of "how many we were going to win by"; that's how it felt.'

Souness set the style by scoring the first goal in each of four early matches, all of which Liverpool won. At Manchester City, Terry McDermott's superb pass found Souness's run through the inside-right channel, and as a City defender moved into challenge, Souness promptly hooked home an angled half-volley from about 20 yards. He got another in the second half, driving home with his left foot after being put in by a Dalglish flick, as Liverpool romped to a 4–1 win. By the time their 5–0 home win over Derby in October came round, Liverpool had hit 33 goals in ten matches and conceded just four. Spurs suffered the most, with that punishing 7–0 defeat, but Norwich City were hit for six in February as Liverpool headed inexorably towards their 85-goal total and their most impressive Championship victory to date.

In a video I have of that time there is a sequence in which that 1978–79 team is coming out up the steps at Anfield before a game with the same sort of swagger that international rugby players deploy after their dressing-room war-dances and psychological pump-ups. But, as we've heard, Liverpool were never gung-ho in dressing-rooms – quite the opposite in fact – so what we are really seeing as the players hurl themselves onto the pitch is not some synthetic self-confidence but the real thing: 11 young men at the height of their powers and hungry for victory. Souness is right there in the middle, of course.

'We were the best. Though I played in great sides in all my seven seasons, if you forced me to choose I'd have to say that team had to be the best. Nealy, Kenny, Ray Kennedy, Big Al, Clem, Jimmy Case; we were so together as a team, so self-motivating, we just hated losing.'

Nevertheless, losses there were, most notably to United in an FA Cup semi-final replay, at Goodison Park of all places, which probably denied that team a Double, because they'd have met Arsenal in the final . . . But the league was won again in 1980, although Souness somehow managed only one goal out of the 81 scored in the season.

Terry McDermott's running was at its height that year, as he notched 11 goals, so that may explain Souness's preference for anchoring the midfield, which he did with a ferocity which made him probably the most feared footballer in the country. This wasn't done in the posturing, chest-beating style of a Vinnie Jones, or with the whirling dervish lunges of a Roy Keane. Souness had only to radiate menace, with those muscular legs and that eyeballing glare letting anyone who fancied their chances know that if they tried to get past him, or take the piss, they would get hurt, not necessarily by foul play but by the sheer physical intensity of his challenges. I think I'm right in saying that he was never sent off in a Liverpool jersey. Indeed, in his six full seasons, Souness only missed 20 League games out of a possible 252, which doesn't indicate a high level of suspensions – nor indeed injuries. But, as Hollywood producer Sam Goldwyn said of ulcers, 'I don't get 'em, I give 'em.'

'Graeme was like our minder,' Terry McDermott says. 'If anybody on the opposite side started saying things during a game, he'd soon sort them out. He was hard but fair . . . most of the time. He was great to have on the pitch because if anyone wanted to mix it, they had to contend with him, and Graeme wouldn't mess around.'

The 1980–81 season now saw Souness assert himself in Europe, with a series of spectacular performances on Liverpool's run to the final in Paris. He scored his first hat-trick as Liverpool overwhelmed Oulu Palloseura 10–1 at Anfield, and then repeated the feat in style against the Bulgarian champions CSKA Sofia. His three goals in the 5–1 first leg win at Anfield on 4 March 1981 came courtesy of some of the most powerful shooting ever seen at the ground, all hit from around the edge of the box, all unstoppable. Souness missed the first leg of the semi-final against Bayern Munich, which saw the Germans take the distinct advantage of a goalless draw back to the Olympic Stadium for the return.

A big crowd and difficult circumstances for the team made an ideal stage for Souness. Quite apart from failing to score at home, Liverpool were now without two key defenders, Phil Thompson and

Alan Kennedy, with the inexperienced Richard Money and Colin Irwin taking their places. To make matters worse, Kenny Dalglish was substituted after being kicked on the ankle inside the first five minutes. It was, as they often say in football, 'a backs to the wall job', but one with some glorious flourishes. Sammy Lee tracked Paul Breitner into near oblivion; Howard Gayle, on for Kenny, produced a thrilling cameo as he ran at the German defence with astonishing verve; and Souness patrolled the area in front of the defence like one of the German police's schnauzer dogs. But Liverpool still needed a goal, and it came just seven minutes from time when the limping David Johnson managed to cross for Ray Kennedy who controlled a difficult ball on his chest before rifling home a right-foot volley. Bayern's equaliser was too late to save them, and a defiant Liverpool went through to the final, where a cautious Real Madrid were defeated by Alan Kennedy's goal nine minutes from time. Souness, like his Scottish colleagues Hansen and Dalglish, now had a second European Cup winner's medal inside three seasons.

Despite that, it had been obvious from the team's league form that the goals were drying up a little – just 62 against their usual 80-odd. With Clemence departing, more changes were inevitable, and there was a rocky first half to the next season, 1981–82, as the new players struggled to give the team its familiar rhythm. Captain Phil Thompson seemed strangely muted, and Bob Paisley, ever alert for fine tuning, began to look elsewhere for leadership. Graeme Souness recalls the manager's approach.

'Phil Thompson hadn't been making too good a job of it, to be frank, but I'd never thought about the captaincy. He felt that I'd touted myself for it, but nothing could be further from the truth. I was standing watching shooting practice one day at Melwood – I had a bit of an ankle injury at the time, so I was just leaning against a goalpost – and Bob came up to me and said, "Would you like to be captain?" And I said, "Well, I'd love to be, but I think there's a few people in front of me." There'd been rumours in the dressing-room about a change, and Phil had been asked on several occasions by Bob if the captaincy was too much for him. When we lost at home to Manchester City on Boxing Day, we were down to 12th in the league. So it was coming. Then I told Bob I'd do it, provided it didn't upset anybody, and he just said that that would be his problem.'

Souness, picked ahead of Dalglish and Hansen to name but two likely candidates, proved to be an inspired and inspiring choice. From the turn of the year Liverpool won 20 of their 25 matches, losing only twice, a run that brought them yet another Championship. Souness contributed goals in wins over Coventry City (4–0), Leeds United (2–0), Stoke City (1–5) and also in a decisive 3–1 victory at Everton.

Ian Rush was also starting to score freely, and he testifies to the Graeme Souness effect in the dressing-room. 'Graeme used to go round to every player at half-time, with his fist clenched, telling us the game was ours to win. He pumped adrenalin into us, and we used to go back out feeling that we couldn't lose. That was the Souness psychology.'

On Saturday, 15 May, after beating Spurs 3–1 at Anfield, the new captain hoisted the Championship trophy one-handed, as if it were the severed head of a defeated opponent. As well as this major honour, he had earlier been able to lift the League Cup (now ludicrously renamed the Milk Cup after sponsorship, the only relief being that a tea company didn't get involved) when Liverpool also beat Spurs 3–1 at Wembley in March.

Liverpool completed the same double under Souness's leadership the following season, the two highlights of which were the 5–0 win at Everton, and the defeat of Manchester United, 2–1 in extra-time, in the League Cup at Wembley. Souness reached his highest total of league goals with nine, scoring an absolute cracker in the 3–1 win at Luton, when he hit the ball with his left foot into the far corner from 25 yards out. It didn't seem like a particularly easy season for Liverpool, but looking back at some of the teams who were then in the First Division – Birmingham City, Swansea City, Notts County, Brighton, Stoke City and Watford – it probably wasn't one of the strongest years. In fact, Liverpool were even able to lose five of their last six games and still finish on 81 points, 11 clear of nearest challengers Watford. Only the bathos of a fifth-round home defeat to Brighton in the FA Cup, and a third round exit from the European Cup to Widzew Lodz, spoiled what was Bob Paisley's last year in charge at Liverpool. And who can forget the thoughtfulness of Souness's gesture, apparently spontaneous, to send Bob Paisley up the steps at Wembley first to collect the League Cup?

The promotion of Joe Fagan, who'd been at the club since the early Bill Shankly days as a trainer and reserve-team coach, might have looked like a gamble from the outside – Fagan had not been the greatest of players, even for Manchester City – but the transition proved seamless, as Souness recalls: 'After Bob's retirement, nothing changed. Training stayed exactly the same. Joe had the same outlook on the game as Bob, and some of the same tricks. He always tried to gee us up by suggesting we weren't as good as previous players and teams, and he was always throwing things in to try and get us going.'

The bare facts of Fagan's first season suggest that everything was in better-than-working order. He had a pretty settled first team, comprising Grobbelaar, Neal, Lawrenson, Hansen, Alan Kennedy, Lee, Souness, Craig Johnston, Ronnie Whelan, Dalglish and Rush, with more than useful back-ups in Steve Nicol, Michael Robinson and later, John Wark. It needed a strong squad to get them through the 66 games they played, in which Souness led them to the Championship, the League Cup and the European Cup, a treble that's unlikely to be repeated by any club.

'In that season we had become, a little bit, a team who could grind out results, we were so organised and so disciplined. Rushie at that time was having the best period of his career, and we'd just go away to places and make sure we didn't concede anything while Rushie would sneak a goal. I felt we weren't playing our best football, but we were maybe more difficult to beat than many of the previous teams.'

Rush was indeed a star turn that year with a haul of 48 goals in 64 appearances, but more of that later. Ironically, in view of Rush's consistent tormenting of Everton, it was a Souness goal which won us the League Cup in the replay at Maine Road, after the first all-Merseyside Wembley final had ended in a goalless draw. Spinning onto a pass on the edge of the Everton area, Souness despatched a left-foot shot into the bottom right-hand corner after 21 minutes.

But the Scot's most potent form was saved for Europe, where Liverpool were unbeaten, home or away, *en route* to the final against Roma. True, they looked to be going out after Athletic Bilbao had held Liverpool to a goalless draw at Anfield in the second-round first leg in October, but an utterly professional performance in the away leg meant that all the Basques were put into one exit, so to speak. Souness recalls the game with relish: 'We were absolutely outstanding. That match and the final were probably the two best games I played for Liverpool. I can remember Evo [Roy Evans] coming into our room on the afternoon of the game to wake us up [Souness shared with Kenny Dalglish] and we said to him, "If we do this lot tonight, we'll win the trophy." We'd trained on the pitch the night before and it was a nice, tight, English-style stadium, with a great atmosphere, but when we got there for the game, they'd soaked the pitch to try and swing things their way. But what they didn't realise was that it couldn't be better for us. The ball was flying around, and that was perfect for that Liverpool team, because the ball was moving quickly. And when things are happening quickly, lesser players can't control it, the ball's away from them. But for good players, like we were, it's there, controlled, and it's happening that yard quicker. So we went out and we were absolutely outstanding, passing right through them.'

Liverpool won by way of a rare headed goal from Ian Rush after 66 minutes, and then returned to the Spanish peninsula to take on the Portuguese champions, Benfica, after beating them at Anfield, also by a single Rush goal, this time after 67 minutes. What kept him?

Another startling performance saw Liverpool win 4–1 in the Stadium of Light, with two from Ronnie Whelan, one from Johnston and another, inevitably, from Rush. They then faced the rugged but skilful Bulgarian champions Dinamo Bucharest, who turned in a battling performance, in both senses, at Anfield, only to lose by a single Sammy Lee goal. The Bulgarian captain, Lica Movila, who either hadn't heard or was insanely brave, decided to mix it with Souness in a big way at Anfield, and ended up being carried off with a broken jaw. Souness puts the case for the defence: 'He'd been elbowing me and threatening me all through game, pulling my shirt, and I think a bit of frustration set in because I ended up chinning him. I never got caught – it'd be a bit more difficult today with all the cameras. I wasn't proud of it, but at the end of the day it was one of those things that happens. And then, coming off the pitch at the end of the game, another of their guys came up and threatened me, and Ronnie Moran got in between us to separate us, while the one with the broken jaw was standing with a great big towel with ice packed in it, wrapped around his face, and tied in a giant bow above his head. I couldn't help laughing at the poor bugger. So the second leg was difficult because they were all after me. We were given a rough time at the airport and I got booed as soon as I walked on the pitch. It was quite exciting because I was kicked all over the place in the game, but we still done the business.'

Alan Hansen remembers Souness coming off the pitch 'with both his socks absolutely shredded where the Romanians had hacked at him', but by this time Ian Rush's two splendid goals had taken any pain away and put Liverpool into the final in Rome on a 3–1 aggregate.

Despite their four wins away from home – they'd also beaten BK Odense 1–0 in the first round – Liverpool were plainly up against it playing AS Roma on their own ground. Their form had been equally impressive, beating IFK Gothenburg, CSKA Sofia, Dynamo Berlin and, er, Dundee United, on the way to what all the Italian press presumed would be a home victory in front of 70,000 supporters. But seven years on from their first European Cup victory in Rome, Liverpool were determined to put up a good show.

A heavy work-load and, yes, the suspicion that we were in for a beating, prevented me from going, an act of cowardice I regret to this day. But by this time in my supporting life, I'd also become something of a 'dead albatross' to Liverpool, somehow managing to turn up at those games they lost. My brother Keith was convinced that my presence would 'put the mockers' on the team, so my absence from Rome may have been the key factor in the victory.

Graeme Souness, who had by now decided to sign for Sampdoria

– 'it was forced on me a bit because my wife at that time had to move abroad for tax reasons' – was doubly on display that night, to the fans he was leaving, and to those who would be judging him next. A win would impress both camps, and Liverpool set about it in minimalist style.

'It was so typical of that group of Liverpool players that we had a meeting almost without discussing Roma. We didn't know their names, hadn't watched them on video. We'd had our lunch on the day of the game, and afterwards Joe Fagan said, "Okay, you've got a big game tonight, and I tell you what, they must be a good team because they're in this final. But they're not as good as you. Now the bus is going to leave at five, so go to your beds and rest." And that was it! When we got to the Olympic Stadium, which was already three-quarters full of Roma fans, I tried to walk round in front of their supporters, just to show them we weren't scared, but the police wouldn't let us go to their end.'

Liverpool's confident demeanour in the preliminaries and during the early stages of the game had both Roma and their fans on edge. When Phil Neal poked home a goal after just 14 minutes, the Italians' nerve began to desert them. This was a team containing several Italian internationals, and the Brazilian midfield player Roberto Falcao, who had been one of the star performers in the 1982 World Cup in Spain. But Souness and Liverpool began to boss them, despite conceding an equaliser before half-time from Pruzzo's looping header. The second half became a tense affair with Roma seemingly content to play for a draw and extra-time.

Souness sensed their defeatism. 'They were holding on in the end. There were a couple of incidents where the ball had gone out of play and their goalkeeper, Tancredi, was telling the ballboys not to run for it. They were wanting extra-time because we'd just passed them out of it. In extra-time there was only one winner, because that Liverpool team had done it so often before. We just kept passing and passing. And, in the end, for the penalties, their bottle had just gone.'

Souness himself scored our third penalty after Steve Nicol had missed the first and Phil Neal had tucked away our second, as the shoot-out edged inexorably towards Alan Kennedy's greatest test of character. We all know now about Bruce Grobbelaar's wobbly-legs routine and Kennedy's successful penalty, but what seems clear is that Liverpool won this final as much with their minds as with their feet. So Souness, who with Dalglish had the strongest will of all, lifted the trophy, and like Kevin Keegan before him, left the club on a great note, with a further 650,000 of them coming from Sampdoria.

Liverpool never fully succeeded in replacing him. Jan Molby and Steve McMahon almost made it as a pair, but the team for much of the 1990s has lacked someone who could combine Souness's passing talent with his ability to intimidate opponents. Even Paul Ince, for all his menace, will probably struggle to fill the Souness role, which goes to show just how unique a player the Scot was.

That should have been the end of the interview but Graeme wanted to keep talking football. So I asked him if his experience with Sampdoria had in any way lessened his appreciation of Liverpool and got a disbelieving snort.

'What going there did was to make me appreciate Liverpool even more. For the first time, at 31, I began to become opinionated about what we'd done. I could point out things in training, and say that I'd done them another way at Liverpool, and it had worked because we'd won all those trophies. I was forming my own opinions, yet the coach at Sampdoria at the time was a really good one, so it wasn't being disrespectful to him. I just had all this experience stacked up. What I liked about Italy, apart from the diet and the climate, was the tolerance level of the supporters. They'd grown used to the more patient style, players just getting on the ball and passing it around. And, funnily enough, the only club in England where the crowd had become educated to this was Liverpool. English football has always been played for entertainment, box to box, whereas on the continent it's more like chess, which is why Liverpool were so successful in Europe.'

I hadn't intended to ask Souness about his time as Liverpool manager, since it came outside the strict remit of the book, but the conversation inevitably drifted into the subject without too much effort by either party. Souness had given up a fortune to leave Rangers when he came to Liverpool to succeed Kenny Dalglish in 1991, because managing Liverpool was the only job in football that he really, really wanted. It seemed like the perfect choice too – a bright, passionate man committed to the Liverpool cause, with a playing record second to none. No first team could point a finger at Graeme Souness and say 'show us your medals'. So why did it go wrong?

'The big danger, when you've had so much success as a player, is that managing the same club drives you crazy because you can't get the players to do what you might have done when you were one of them. And so it all came down to me not being able to understand why those players didn't share the same passion that I'd had. I fell out badly with some of the older players, because they couldn't get to that kind of pitch of emotion. And they done me in the end. Well, I done myself as well. In terms of football, they were still as good as anybody, but introduce a bit of aggro and they were the worst. And I used to ask them to think about what the manager in the other dressing-room would be saying – "Let's go out and play football against Liverpool", or "Let's go out and get stuck into them"? I'm sure Roy Evans feels the same as I did now. If you take the 1996 Cup final against Manchester United, Roy Keane just ran the show. He's gone through a couple of people early on, and more or less said, "Okay, this is the way it's going to be – anyone fancy it?" I think Robbie Fowler was the only one to square up to him. In the Liverpool teams I played in, we'd have been fighting each other to get to Keane; we'd have been queueing up to take him on.'

Souness's heart operation took place in the spring of 1992, but he was able to make it to Wembley to see the team win the FA Cup, something he'd never achieved as a player, which must have been a touching moment. But the fallout from selling his story to *The Sun* did him a lot of damage. It *was* tactless of him, given what the paper had said about Hillsborough but, at the same time, I never understood why more Liverpool fans hadn't realised what a shitty paper it was beforehand, as though it had never got things wrong or offended public taste before the disaster.

Souness finally left Liverpool – and I suppose we can say that it was for good – in January 1994. For someone who'd given so much to the club, it was a painful way to go. How did we lose two of our most successful and passionate men in a three-year span?

Like Kenny, Graeme is still in the game, unable to give up the buzz. He should enjoy himself a little more in Italy than he was able to do at Southampton, or indeed Liverpool. 'I've got a passion for the game; I love football,' he says. 'When I came back from my operation, I'd fallen out of love with it. Maybe that was me needing time to get over the trauma of the operation, but I love football, and I always will. And, yes, it does drive you mad, and maybe you need to rest from time to time. But you still love it.'

With that, we've finally finished, except that as he stands and stretches before setting off on yet another journey, he suddenly says, 'What memories. I wish I could turn the clock back.' And you suspect that it's said not just for himself, but for Liverpool too.

ALAN KENNEDY

Barney Rubble

The Liverpool fans, and the team itself, quickly nicknamed Alan Kennedy 'Barney Rubble' when he signed for the Reds in August 1978, for a fee of £330,000 from a Newcastle United side that had just been relegated to Division Two. It fitted him perfectly – the small squat figure with an engaging chuckle from *The Flintstones* cartoon series was almost an exact match for the chunky left-back whom Liverpool brought in to take the place of the all-too-briefly famous Joey Jones. The tattooed Jones had become a cult figure with the Kop, with his clenched-fist salutes and bone-shuddering tackles, not to mention his rapport with fans. But his lack of foot-balling finesse was always going to be found out at the higher levels, and after enjoying a wonderful year in the 1976–77 season, when Liverpool took the Championship and their first European Cup, Joey never quite got the magic back the following year, and so, as Liverpool continually had to reshuffle their defence over the latter part of the season, finding a ready-made replacement was always on the cards.

He arrived in the shape of Alan Kennedy, whom many Liverpool fans remembered as the 19-year-old kid who was thrown into New-castle's 1974 FA Cup final side on the morning of the match, after regular defender David Craig had failed a fitness test. Kennedy was deemed by most experts to have been Newcastle's best player on the day, which may not have been saying much given the 3–0 thumping which Liverpool had handed out. But his gutsy performance must have been noted in the Anfield boot-room ledger and his progress monitored by the club's scouting network, for almost as soon as he signed for Liverpool on 14 August, he was out on the Anfield turf performing just five days later in Liverpool's first league game of the season, against Queen's Park Rangers. 'I didn't have time to stop and think about it, really,' Kennedy says of his sudden transition, 'though it helped that my old team-mate Terry McDermott was there. He told me all about the club, but I knew quite a few of the players from my call-up to the England Under-23 squad.'

The match programme for that game offered us a detailed introduction to the Wearsider – never call Alan a Geordie because he was born in Sunderland, though he watched both his home-town team and Newcastle as a boy – with an endorsement from none other than Albert Stubbins, a legendary centre-forward for Liverpool and Newcastle in the 1940s and 1950s:

> When Newcastle were struggling so much, Alan Kennedy could be relied upon to do his stuff. Indeed, for a time, Newcastle switched him to a midfield position where he could be used in an attacking role. One of his great assets as a full-back is that he can set up attacks by going on the overlap. He's cast in the Terry Cooper mould and he can be very effective when he's doing this. In the 1974 final, he was just about the only success in a Newcastle side that had a bad day. It was a last-minute decision as to whether or not he played and, as it turned out, he really justified his selection. Alan is a likeable lad and he's been a loyal club-man. I rate him a certainty to get a full England cap. He's a left-sided player, as Puskas was, but while I'm not making any comparisons, I will say that Alan can do more with one foot than some players can do with two, and the same applied to Puskas and Raich Carter. Alan is strong in the tackle, has good anticipation and is so fast that no winger will beat him for speed. He gets on top of a man and is very hard to shake off. He's got everything going for him and Liverpool can be satisfied they have signed a very fine player.

Puskas comparisons aside, Albert was more or less spot on in his assessment of a player who also went on to attain cult status for Liverpool, not just because of his fearless play but also for scoring four of the most important goals in the club's history. Chris Lawler may have got 61 goals from right-back but I doubt if any full-back in history has scored more vital goals for a club than Alan Kennedy did. It can be, and indeed has been, argued that he won Liverpool four separate trophies – two European Cups and two League Cups – in his seven-and-a-bit seasons with the club. 'He's special,' Kenny Dalglish once said of him, tongue in cheek, 'he only scores in cup finals.' Indeed, when Kennedy turns up at Anfield now on match days in his role as a commentator and phone-in host for BBC Radio Merseyside, he still gets back-slaps and cheers from the stewards in the reception area as he goes about his media business.

Kennedy had joined Newcastle after a tip-off by his older brother, Keith, who had also joined the club. After doing his paper round, he would catch a bus up to Newcastle to train with the youth team and soon signed professional forms. It was partly Keith's move to Bury that helped him get into the first team – and that 1974 final – but the arrival of Bill McGarry in 1977 saw the club go into decline, and soon found Kennedy looking for First Division football.

'I was living in a council house at the time with my sister and my father, who was a diabetic, so I couldn't afford to play in the Second Division,' he recalls. 'I'd also had a bad injury in 1977 – torn medial ligaments which had to be stitched back on to the bone – so I was aware of having to take any opportunity while it lasted. I think Leeds were also interested in me, but after a talk with Terry and Peter Robinson, and my father, Liverpool were the team for me.'

Kennedy was quickly accepted as the real deal by Liverpool fans, as he appeared in the first 20 league games of what was to be a record-breaking season. During that period, from mid-August to mid-December, Liverpool's remodelled defence conceded only nine goals, while the attack rattled up 44. Kennedy 'created' a goal for Dalglish in the 4–1 win at Manchester City, slicing an intended right-foot shot into the unmarked Scot's path, thereby allowing Dalglish to cruise past Joe Corrigan and slide home. But he scored his own first goal for Liverpool two games later, rattling in a left-footer to complete a 3–0 win at Birmingham City on 9 September. With Ray Kennedy immediately in front of him on the left side of midfield, Liverpool's opponents must have felt like the American

Republican party – Kennedys everywhere. 'Bob Paisley had bought me as a defender who could support the midfield – that's what he wanted from me,' Kennedy says. 'But I had a lot of pace as well, and though I was always apprehensive before games, as soon as I got a touch I'd be okay. And I was the type of player who, if I didn't get something right, I'd put it right as soon as I could.'

Ray Clemence, who conceded only 16 goals that season, was among the first to be impressed by the new recruit to his defence: 'Alan was probably not as technically gifted as Alec Lindsay had been, but he was a great character and it soon became apparent that he'd run through brick walls for the team. He had a great left-foot and could get tremendous distance on his clearances and passes, so I knew I could give him the ball with confidence. The Anfield crowd took to him right away because, although he wasn't in the Joey Jones mould of extroverts, they could see that he wore his heart on his sleeve.'

The early disappointment of their League Cup and European Cup exits had a typical effect on Liverpool – they tried harder, ran faster and scored at a furious rate, determined to make up for the early loss of the European crown which they had held for two years.

Kennedy's pace down the left flank and willingness to go on runs were clearly going to be assets for his new team. He was pretty sound defensively too, as the goals-against column suggests, tackling with a ferocity and a speed which belied his lack of height – he was only five foot nine inches tall. He could indeed reduce wingers to rubble, which was another reason his nickname suited him so much.

He scored his second goal of the season in the 6–0 rout of Norwich City at Anfield and, as Liverpool finished off their greatest league season with five wins on the trot, he scored inside the first minute as Aston Villa were beaten 3–0. He missed the two FA Cup semi-final games against Manchester United, which was a blessing because Liverpool lost the replay.

So only one trophy was won in his first season, but it was done in magnificent style. The only blot on the title run-in was Kennedy's unfortunate statement to a newspaper at Easter that the club were 'already Champions'. Liverpool immediately went down to their heaviest defeat of the season, 3–1 at Aston Villa, and Kennedy was promptly reminded in no uncertain terms by Bob Paisley that this wasn't the Liverpool way. 'We'd just beaten Manchester United 2–0 on Easter Saturday, so we were all on a high afterwards,' remembers Kennedy, 'but I must have said something to the press because the next day there were headlines in the papers quoting me saying, "Liverpool are already Champions" – just the sort of thing the Villa lads would bite on. So when we went and lost there on the Easter Monday, Bob went berserk afterwards. I got roasted in the dressing-room – all about Liverpool never shooting their mouths off, or giving opponents something they could use against us. The message was simple – Liverpool saved their talking for on the pitch. It was an early lesson for me on how the club operated.'

Nevertheless, a year after being relegated with Newcastle, Alan Kennedy was now the proud possessor of a League Championship medal. And he doubled his haul of football honours the next season as Liverpool retained their title, undefeated at Anfield. But they were denied in the semi-finals of the two cup competitions, and beaten in the first round of the European Cup by the Georgian champions Dinamo Tbilisi. By Liverpool's high standards, just one trophy a season wasn't enough. It seemed inevitable that Paisley would look to retune the engine in an attempt to return to the performance levels that had conquered Europe. Kennedy had missed a few games at the back end of the season, including the title clincher against Aston Villa at Anfield, being replaced by the Israeli international Avi Cohen. After appearing in the first five games of the next season, in which he scored in wins against Crystal Palace (3–0) and Norwich City (4–1), Kennedy missed several games and he and Cohen began a long battle over the whole of the season for the number 3 shirt, with Kennedy playing 19 times in the league and Cohen 13. 'I didn't mind the competition,' Kennedy says. In theory, it was a situation Paisley would have enjoyed – two players vying for the same position – but changes made because of injuries and fluctuations in form were no substitute for a settled team, playing with purpose and rhythm. Liverpool's league performances suffered accordingly – only 11 wins out of 25 games before Christmas, and then six out of 17 afterwards, with 42 goals conceded, an unusually high total for such a previously solid defence.

Liverpool were also out of the FA Cup by the end of January, beaten in the fourth round by Everton. It looked as though the first blank season since 1974–75 had arrived. Yet, bizarrely, the season was to end with a double triumph, in which Alan Kennedy of all people was directly involved. The club's stealthy progress in the League Cup, past a series of lower-division teams, had suddenly blossomed, in the light of failures elsewhere, into a serious pursuit of a trophy they had never won before. A 1–1 draw in the second leg of the semi-final against Manchester City at Anfield protected the one-goal lead Liverpool had taken from Maine Road, and they now had a March date for the final at Wembley against West Ham. Ironically, in view of their tussle for the left-back position, neither Kennedy nor Cohen played in that second semi-final, the number 3 shirt going instead to Richard Money, who had been bought from Fulham as a reserve defender. But, for the final, on Saturday, 14 March, Kennedy was back in the side, back at Wembley trying to exorcise the ghosts of his losing appearance there in 1974.

'It was a close-fought game, because West Ham had some good players at the time. Once it went into extra-time it looked as though it would be a goalless draw – but then, right near the end, about three minutes from time, we had an attack. I was in the inside-left slot, and the ball came back to me. I didn't have time to think, even though it was on my right foot, so I just hit it. Sammy Lee was lying injured in the West Ham box at the time, and ducked as my shot passed over him and into the net. West Ham thought there should have been an offside, but the goal stood. We thought we'd won, but West Ham got a penalty in the very last seconds and Ray Stewart scored. The Liverpool lads were probably too busy laughing that I'd scored with my right foot.'

There were some supporters and television viewers, mostly Londoners, I suppose, who thought that Lee was actually feigning injury, going to ground because he knew he was offside, and could see Kennedy lining up his shot. But I couldn't possibly comment on that. Liverpool came from a goal down to win the replay at Villa

Park 2–1, and gave the pursuit of the European Cup new momentum. Liverpool had seen off CSKA Sofia on a 6–1 aggregate in the quarter-finals in March, and now faced Bayern Munich in the semis. Kennedy played in the first (goalless) leg at Anfield but, along with Phil Thompson, was injured for the return in Germany. The patched-up defence performed heroically, though, and the 1–1 draw was enough to see Liverpool through to Paris and the final against Real Madrid on 27 May.

Although Richard Money played in six of the final seven league games in the number 3 shirt, Alan Kennedy was able to come back for the last fixture, at home to Manchester City, and prove his fitness, a task that Dalglish was also able to achieve just before the final itself. It was a humid night in Paris, and the Parc des Princes Stadium was ringed by CRS riot police who all looked as though they couldn't wait to get stuck in. Liverpool fans seemed to outnumber their Spanish counterparts by two to one.

Inside the stadium, a great chant of '*Allez les Rouges!*' rang out, not from the neutral French, but from Scousers who'd picked up the rallying cry from the game against St Etienne four years earlier. In the event, the game itself, despite that great early atmosphere, failed to live up to anybody's expectations, including those of the spotty youths with the truncheons. With less than ten minutes to go in the game, my West Brom girlfriend and I were just talking about the inevitability of extra-time when right down below us Ray Kennedy took a long throw, having seen Alan Kennedy's sudden movement from deep. Alan's scurrying run wasn't picked up by the Real Madrid defence, and, as he chested the ball on with great skill, he bullocked his way past a rather feeble tackle to get into the six-yard box. I think most of us in that split-second expected him to square the ball across the Madrid goal, but in another blink of an eye the ball was in the back of the net, put there by Kennedy's inspired decision to go for goal.

'When I made the run onto Ray's throw, it was just spontaneous, we had nothing planned,' he recalls. 'But once I'd got the ball down off my chest I thought I'd keep going. Their defender must have seen me with steam coming out of my ears and decided to give me a miss, because I went right past him, and I just saw the goalkeeper move away from his post, looking for the cross, and I thumped it.'

'It was a marvellous goal, worthy of winning any major tournament,' ace goalscorer Kenny Dalglish said at the time, while Alan Hansen called it 'spectacular', even if there was some delighted surprise in the team about the identity of the scorer.

Those of us who were there were grateful that the stadium had an arc of space behind the goal for the jubilant Kennedy to decelerate in. Had it been a standard English ground, he'd have ended up embedded in Row Z. To the bemusement of the French, a mass cry of 'Bar-ney! Bar-ney!' rang around the Parc des Princes, which might have put the CRS on full alert in other circumstances.

Kennedy now had iconic status because of the goal, with the crowds expectant almost every time he touched the ball that another unlikely run and shot would occur. He managed three goals in the league the following season, as Liverpool reclaimed the Championship after their lapse in 1981. A second-minute strike helped beat Coventry 2–1 away in September, and then, in the spring, he got one inside four minutes in the 2–0 win over Stoke City, having also scored three days earlier in the 5–0 thrashing of Manchester City at Maine Road.

The League Cup was retained with a 3–1 win over Spurs, but CSKA Sofia got some revenge for the previous year's beating, by knocking us out of the European Cup in the third round.

The defensive reshuffles that season – the year that Souness took over as captain in mid-season – saw Mark Lawrenson assimilated, sometimes as centre-half when Kennedy was missing, sometimes as centre-half when Phil Thompson was out, with Phil Neal the only ever-present in the league campaign. But Kennedy's resilience enabled him to hang onto his place the following season – indeed he played in all 42 league matches, getting his usual quota of three goals.

But he also notched another of his big-occasion goals in the League Cup final at Wembley against Manchester United. United had taken a first-half lead through Norman Whiteside and, given their long run of success over us in cup competition, we had few hopes of getting back into the game. But fifteen minutes from time, as United broke up another Liverpool attack on the right wing, first Souness and then Craig Johnston won the ball back, playing it to Sammy Lee who brought the ball into the middle, before seeing Alan Kennedy advance from full-back. With just a touch to control the ball, he took it forward a yard before hitting a scything, 25-yard drive which bounced over Gary Bailey's drive, before bulging into the far corner of the United net. Barney had done it again!

'I'd hit a similar shot earlier, but it went high, so I concentrated on getting it lower and aiming for the corner where any rebound would be picked by Rushie or Kenny. But it bounced and zipped and Bailey was probably done for pace,' Kennedy recalls.

The game duly went into extra-time with Liverpool now on the attack, and Kennedy was again involved in the winning goal. Bringing the ball down the left, he plays the ball to Ronnie Whelan, and continues his run into the United penalty area, either as a decoy, or in the hope of getting a return pass. But Whelan tries a cross and finds it rebounding back to him. Kennedy, sensing that he is offside, immediately back-pedals, and, in that instant, Whelan curls a wonderful shot beyond Bailey into the far side of the goal, one defender having been taken out of the play by Kennedy's run. The victory allowed Bob Paisley to make the first of his grand exits at Wembley.

With the title also claimed again, the only problem Kennedy faced was the possibility that new manager Joe Fagan might not fancy him as his left-back. But the changes Fagan wrought were up front and in midfield, as Michael Robinson was brought in as an auxiliary forward, and later John Wark as an attacking midfielder. Steve Nicol, a player who appeared as comfortable in midfield as in defence, was also on the upgrade, but once again Kennedy held his position throughout the season, appearing in all 42 league games, as the Neal, Hansen, Lawrenson and Kennedy back-four assumed a rock-like solidity. Only Neal missed a single game that year.

With such defensive stability, it was hardly surprising that Liverpool should have a successful season, but nobody could have guessed that it would be so fruitful. The League Cup was claimed for the fourth season running, with Kennedy playing in all 13 ties – but not, for once, scoring any goals. He was also an ever-present in the European Cup campaign which, by the end of April, had taken Liverpool to their fourth final. But, again, he didn't score. On the final run to Liverpool's 15th Championship, however, he notched two, the best of which was a wonderfully athletic volley, hit on the run in the 2–2 draw at home to Ipswich – 'probably my best in terms of technique, though not in importance. They were a good side, Ipswich'.

And so to Rome. We have heard how Liverpool were in a relaxed state of mind for the trip, no doubt helped by having two trophies in the bag already, and perhaps by the thought that even if they lost to Roma in Rome, nobody could criticise them in such heavily loaded circumstances. But Alan Hansen remembers that there was 'almost a premonition as we trained at Melwood that the final would go right down to a penalty shoot-out'.

Two sets of penalty shoot-outs were apparently practised, one with reserves and youth-team players taking spot-kicks against Bruce Grobbelaar, while each first-team player took penalties against one of the junior keepers. Hansen remembers the near-farce that ensued: 'The youth team stuck all five penalties past Bruce while, I swear to you, not one of us first-teamers could get one in. Nobody was taking it lightly, but they just couldn't score. And, of course, the worst offender seemed to be Alan Kennedy. He must have had a dozen tries and kept hitting the ball wide!'

Kennedy remembers this slightly differently: 'I did score a few, but there was no goalie in the net at the time. I don't think anyone seriously thought that I'd take one if it came to it, anyway.'

This may have been because on the only two occasions that Kennedy had taken penalties in matches – pre-season games in Germany and Spain – he had missed both of them. But here he was, insisting that he should be one of the five chosen for a shoot-out if the Rome final came down to it, even if the rest didn't believe him.

Of course what we don't know here is which of the players had ruled themselves out in such an eventuality. Alan Hansen freely admits that he 'wouldn't volunteer for the job', and there must have been others who decided against it, effectively allowing the brave but unreliable Kennedy to make the short-list on the night.

Kenny Dalglish would not have been one of these but, having been substituted during the game proper, he was not allowed to be a penalty-taker after it. So, as the final minutes of extra-time ticked away, with Roma apparently happy to settle for the shoot-out, the tension among those who had volunteered must have been enormous. I can remember doing some calculations as I watched the game on telly, trying to work out who the five would be – I had Rush, Souness and Phil Neal down as certainties. But I couldn't guess who the others might be – Ronnie Whelan, perhaps, or Mark Lawrenson? It was much the same for Kennedy.

The picture became even more confusing when Steve Nicol marched out of the crowded centre-circle to take the first, and promptly blasted the ball over the bar. When di Bartolomei scored to put Roma ahead, I was ready to hide behind the sofa. But then Mr Reliable, Phil Neal, scored our second, as coolly as he had done in the same stadium seven years earlier. Now Bruno Conti missed in similar fashion to Nicol, to leave it at 1–1. Graeme Souness scored from the third kick to give us the lead, and then Righetti equalised. Rushie put us back ahead, 3–2. And now Brucie was doing his jelly legs number as Graziani placed the ball on the spot. He ran in and fired the ball against the top of the bar and over, to leave Liverpool 3–2 ahead. The Italians had only one penalty left so if we could score the next, we'd have it won. And as Alan Kennedy moved out of the centre-circle, I admit it, I covered my eyes. Kennedy now provides the pictures.

'We were all stood in the centre-circle, and we knew that Phil Neal, Souness and Rushie were certs, but then Joe Fagan began looking around and he said, "Alan, are you all right?" and I said yes, not understanding what he wanted. When it became obvious, I thought, "What have I done here? Me taking the fifth penalty!" When it came to my kick, being useless at additions, I was trying to work out what it meant if I scored or missed. I could see the looks on the players' faces, not fancying my chances – especially Hansen! So I set off, wondering what they were all doing behind my back.

And I just thought I must hit the target, and I did a little dummy just as I ran up, and put it in the other side.'

Barney could be relied upon for a blaster, but this had required nerves of steel, a placement perhaps, something cute to fox Tancredi in the Roma goal. As I peered through my fingers, Kennedy was placing the ball on the spot. He backed away, wiping his hands on his shorts – why, was he going to punch it in? – and then advanced on the ball. I closed my eyes again and let the commentator Brian Moore tell me he'd done it. When I opened them, Barney was doing a little war-dance of delight back to his team-mates who engulfed him in joy. When they showed the replay, I could watch it, relaxed, and appreciate all the technique and coolness which had allowed Kennedy to side-foot the ball inside the left-hand post.

Inevitably, after such a high, the rest of Kennedy's playing career with Liverpool wandered into anticlimax. He dropped out of the team with an injury in March the following year as Liverpool vainly battled Everton for the Championship. He got just one goal – in a 3–1 defeat at Arsenal – and missed the FA Cup semi-final and its replay against Manchester United as Jim Beglin claimed his place.

He also missed the ill-fated European Cup final against Juventus in Brussels. He played in the first eight games of Dalglish's first season as player-manager, but Beglin then became first choice and Kennedy slipped away to his home-town club, Sunderland, to finish his playing career. It didn't work out too well, and he returned to Merseyside when it was all over. He now lives near Ormskirk, organising his busy career for local radio programmes and as a host of junior football tournaments. He also occasionally acts as a guide for one of those package tours of Anfield and Melwood which the club and its commercial connections now organise. He is himself, technically, one of the most famous exhibits – the man whose left foot won two European Cup finals. Maybe Albert Stubbins was right to compare Kennedy to Puskas after all.

IAN RUSH

Goal Machine

If, as a simple question in a pub quiz, you were to be asked who scored 346 goals in 658 appearances for one English football club, you would almost certainly get the answer as quick as the player's goalscoring reflexes: Ian Rush. If you were asked which teenager joined Liverpool in 1980 from a Third Division team for a record £300,000, you might hesitate a little. For, as we have heard from Alan Hansen, Liverpool made a habit of buying up cheapish, unknown young footballers towards the end of each season as a means of avoiding paying unnecessary tax on profits, and more of these players failed than succeeded. So you could have answered, say, 'Kevin Sheedy' to that question and been nearly right.

The right answer was, of course, Ian Rush again. But the element of doubt in your mind underlines the fact that, more than any other Liverpool player in recent history, Ian Rush is defined by his goals. He hasn't appeared in potato crisp adverts, he hasn't modelled clothes, he hasn't appeared on *Have I Got News For You*, he hasn't been an expert analyser for televised football. No, Ian Rush just scores goals.

So let's define him further: 229 goals in the league, just 16 behind Liverpool's holder of that particular record, Roger Hunt; 39 goals in the FA Cup, including five in three finals, making him the highest scorer in the competition's history; 49 goals in the League Cup, just one behind record-holder Geoff Hurst of West Ham; and 20 goals in European competitions for Liverpool, a total that might have been trebled had it not been for the Heysel Stadium disaster and the ensuing six-year ban on Liverpool. There were a further three goals in Charity Shield games, and seven in the weird Screen Sport Super

Cup, a competition which was designed (but which failed) to take the place of European contests. And then there's perhaps the most punishing statistic of all if you belong to the blue half of the city of Liverpool: Rush scored 25 goals against Everton, more than any other player, including the legendary Dixie Dean, in matches between the two Merseyside teams.

Gary Lineker, who played in three such matches during his single season with Everton in 1985–86, readily pays tribute to the man who almost single-handedly made sure that his stay on Merseyside was trophy-free: 'Ian was very similar to myself in that he wasn't a great player outside the area. But he was just a terrific goalscorer, and a big-occasion finisher as well. Two goals in each of the Liverpool v Everton FA Cup finals showed that. He was frighteningly sharp in his heyday. He always seemed in control when he got a chance, never over-excited, never "rushed", as it were. But he was also a great defender as well, the way he pressurised the opposition defence as soon as they got the ball. But I think this may have led to a few problems in his career. It's all right doing it when you're 21 or so, but not when you're 27 or 28. When I went to Barcelona and started chasing defenders, they said, "Stop that, we want to save your energy for scoring," and I thought, "Great, I'll have some of that!" It was a pity Rushie couldn't let himself have, or wasn't allowed, the same leeway, because it's all very well him being a great defensive forward, but I think by doing that he lost an element of what he was really about, which was simply scoring goals.'

Rush had scored 14 goals in 34 appearances for Chester before he was picked up by Liverpool in April 1980 as an 18-year-old, having pulled out of signing for them a month earlier. Rush was the youngest of ten children in his family, whose dependency on their father's employment at Shotton steelworks was always in the balance because of the plant's dubious future. The Rush family home was on a council estate in Flint, a small town on the North Wales coast overlooking the Dee estuary, and a place that Liverpudlians would pass, but never stop at, on their way to the resorts of Prestatyn, Rhyl or Colwyn Bay. Any kid from Flint growing into teenage years would seek out action in Chester or Liverpool, rather than in the town itself. If you said 'Flint' even to Scousers, they would wrinkle their noses, because it seemed a 'white trash' sort of place, with nothing going for it. But then all that stretch of the North Wales coast was utterly patronised by Scousers through the ages. When I was a fairly serious Mod – younger readers had better ask their dads for an explanation – in the mid-1960s, I travelled, as a junior member, with a mohair-suited gang from our local Huyton disco one weekend through most of those North Wales resorts. We posed, which was the Mod's first duty, we laughed at the clothes on the North Waleian lads, and we tried to smooth in with their women at the clubs. Anyone who got in our way was seen off. No wonder Welsh nationalism flourished in these parts as a means of identity and fighting back.

Ian Rush's salvation in his formative years was simply football. He played for his school team, his area team, a Welsh schools Under-15 team, even a Great Britain Catholic Schools XI. Joining Chester as an apprentice in 1978 on £16 per week would probably have been enough of an escape even if he hadn't gone on to Liverpool two years later. An FA Cup run to the fifth round with Chester in 1980 brought him a bonus of £150, which he spent on his first car – a Hillman Avenger, no less – but when he signed for Liverpool he was suddenly in late-registered Ford territory on £300 per week.

But the money didn't change Rush enough to stop him getting slaughtered by the other players when he arrived at Melwood in his rusting Avenger, jeans and T-shirt, and with his bum-fluff moustache. And it went on and on, led chiefly by Kenny Dalglish, whom the unhappy Rush came to loathe at that time for his jibes. 'It was all part of the growing-up process, though I didn't like it at the time. I was getting changed between Alan Hansen and Ray Clemence so I was a bit in awe. I felt as though I shouldn't have been there. And, if you're quiet, that's when the mickey-taking starts. But it helped me settle down eventually.'

Rush played a few reserve games at the back of that season and remembers that among the players in the team were the likes of Steve Ogrizovic, Kevin Sheedy, Alan Harper, Howard Gayle and Colin Irwin, all of whom had to move away from Liverpool to make a career in football. The fact that Liverpool had splashed out such a large sum of money on Rush's unproven talent only made him more uncomfortable, and his first full season with the reserves wasn't much happier. 'I'd given myself a two-year target to get into the first team but after three to four months I thought I was good enough. The problem was that I was trying to play too much for the team in training rather than being selfish and scoring goals.'

Alan Hansen says that his early impressions of Rush were not favourable: 'He couldn't head a ball, he couldn't score, and I though he'd be on his way. Another good tip of mine!' Graeme Souness confirms that 'Rushie never showed much in his early days. He came across a bit shy and awkward, and it showed on the pitch.'

Liverpool fans should fast-forward a little here to the fates of Wayne Harrison and Lee Jones, two young strikers signed up by Liverpool for largish fees in the 1990s, but who never made the grade despite their apparent promise. Rush was in exactly that category in his first season, burdened with expectation thanks to a price-tag not of his own making, and yet lacking the sophistication and perhaps the help, to make sure that he justified the money. As we have heard, Liverpool never coached, they just threw young players into the rough waters of the five-a-side games and the reserve matches and those that swam made it. Those that didn't had to go elsewhere to make a name – the fact that many of those Rush played with in the stiffs *did* succeed eventually, shows not only that the potential was there, but also that Liverpool were ruthless about their high standards of expectancy.

Rush at least got some early encouragement when he was picked for his first-team début for the away game at Ipswich Town on 13 December 1980. He stood in for Dalglish of all people, and wore the famous number 7 shirt. 'It ended up with little Sammy Lee playing up front alongside me and he yattered to me all the time.' The game ended in an uneventful 1–1 draw with Jimmy Case getting our goal. This was the season when Liverpool 'slumped' to fifth place in the league, and Rush was promptly dropped back to the reserves.

But it was also the season when Liverpool were marching on two cups in the spring – the League Cup and the European Cup – so any injuries or tiredness could see a youngster thrown in for an important game. For Ian Rush, the chance game when David Johnson – a man who always seemed to be playing with a black eye, for some reason – was injured between the drawn League Cup final against West Ham at Wembley on 14 March and the replay at Villa Park on 1 April. So Rush got the number 9 shirt this time, and had a part in the Dalglish goal, crisply coming off his defender and laying off a pass to Terry McDermott, whose chip Dalglish hooked home. It was a small but relevant cameo of Rush's ability. He got back into the team for six more league games at the end of the season, but didn't score as Liverpool had long since let their Championship challenge drift away.

However, he was picked for the first leg of the European Cup semi-final against Bayern Munich at Anfield, which ended in a frustrating goalless draw. Nevertheless, once Liverpool had got through to the final in Paris, Paisley included Rush in the 18-strong party to travel. The manager had, according to Rush, 'promised that I would be involved', but in the end the involvement went no further than sitting in the Parc des Princes stands, as Rush and Avi Cohen were not even chosen to be among the five permitted substitutes. No doubt Bob Paisley told him 'I know how you feel', but it was little consolation at the time. 'I was very disappointed by his decision. I thought I was worth a place on the bench.'

Rush's resentment of Bob Paisley's action spilled over into a transfer request and a prolonged row over pay at the beginning of the next season, when the striker once again found himself starting in the reserves, as Bruce Grobbelaar and new signing Mark Lawrenson went straight into the first team where they were soon joined by Rush's Irish reserve-team buddy Ronnie Whelan. Of course the row was only superficially about money; the real subtext was Rush's future at the club. Rush thought he was ready for the first team on a regular basis, while Paisley pointed to the fact that the player hadn't managed a single senior goal yet. Fortunately, his first strike wasn't long in coming.

On as a substitute in the home tie against Finnish side Oulu Palloseura on 30 September 1981, with Liverpool already 4–0 up, Rush slotted home the fifth goal, before Mark Lawrenson and Terry

McDermott added two more. It didn't matter that the Finns were a largely amateur outfit, Ian Rush now had his name in Liverpool's goalscoring book. On 7 October he scored twice against Exeter City in the first leg of a League Cup tie, followed three days later by his first two league goals, against Leeds United in a 3–0 win at Anfield. He got another two against Exeter in the away leg on 28 October, another European Cup goal against AZ Alkmaar on 4 November, and then his first goal against Everton in the 3–1 win at Anfield on 7 November. 'I was playing to get away, really, because I was still angry with Paisley. But once he'd seen me start to score goals, he was suddenly all right with me. He told me that he hadn't even passed my transfer request to the board.'

Ian Rush finally had what the American sports coaches call 'the big mo'' (momentum), and his name was on everybody's lips. In just over a month he had gone from sulking teenager to Liverpool's 'new goal machine', as the northern tabloids like to call him. Nobody could have known it then, but the template he had established in the month of his 20th birthday – goals in the league, the League Cup and the European Cup, and against Everton – was almost a DNA sample of his career to come. Ian Rush was going to get goals in every competition he played in. By Christmas he had been awarded his disputed pay-rise.

Rush appeared 32 times for Liverpool in the league that season, scoring 17 goals. He also scored two in Europe, three in the FA Cup, and eight in the League Cup, including the last in a 3–1 win over Spurs on 13 March 1982 in the final at Wembley.

Liverpool's remarkable turnaround in league form after Christmas – 20 wins in 25 games – under new captain Graeme Souness, also swept them to the title with 87 points. Rush scored 14 goals in this spell, including his first hat-trick, in a 4–0 away win against Notts County. 'I'd got two goals and Souness was still shouting at me to get more – that was the kind of leader he was, because I probably wouldn't have got the hat-trick without him geeing me up.' With Ronnie Whelan now on the left side of midfield and Rush up front, there had been a sudden transfusion of youth and pace into the team. I can remember seeing Rush's goal at Arsenal that May, as

Whelan broke out of defence at speed, before finding Rush, and Ian just accelerated in from the left wing past all the Arsenal defenders – and they were young in those days – before curling a shot into the far top corner for a classic counter-attacking goal. It was a style that was to terrify defences both at home and in Europe over the next four seasons, because Rush now had a taste for both goals and success, and had the self-confidence to achieve them. Two winner's medals at the end of his first full season had seen to that.

Season 1982–83 was Bob Paisley's last in charge of Liverpool, and although Rush had not felt much empathy or warmth from the gaffer when he'd first arrived, he had come to appreciate that the toughening-up process, the blows to the ego, the lack of direct praise, were all part of Liverpool's character-building processes.

But Rush was to prove beyond doubt in this season that not only had Paisley's original judgement about his football potential been right, but also his approach to getting the best out of the youngster. Fed by the intuitive passes and flicks of Kenny Dalglish, who had finally found a player whose physical speed matched that of his own mental agility, Rush, to borrow Ron Atkinson's favourite phrase, 'scored for fun' that season. He managed 24 goals in the league in just 34 appearances, while Dalglish chipped in with 18 of his own to help the club take a second consecutive title. And though the FA Cup and the European Cup both turned out to be anticlimaxes that year, Liverpool were still able to claim the League Cup for the third year running, beating Manchester United at Wembley in extra-time.

And then there was Everton. It is now well documented that Rush did to Everton what green kryptonite did to Superman – not that Everton should be compared to mythical heroes with astonishing powers because that would be wholly inaccurate for obvious reasons. But 6 November 1982 was where the real humiliation began, and at Goodison Park too. I've already described how Alan Hansen set up the first of Rush's four goals that day in the 11th minute, so let's look at the remaining three, all in the second half, with Everton theoretically still in the game at only 1–0 down.

Alan Hansen has encroached into the Everton half, the ball at his feet. He sees a pass to Rush on the edge of the area, but then stops to turn away from a challenge. Meanwhile, Rush has made another run to lose his marker. Hansen passes to Rush's feet as he cuts in from the right, and then, as Rush is about to be tackled by two defenders, he cleverly hits it against one of their legs with his left foot to send the ball inside the post. All right, it was a lucky deflection, but it may have gone in anyway.

Next, Dalglish gets the ball just on the Liverpool side of the half-way line. The Everton defence has pushed right up, and Rush is instantly leaning at what looks like a 45-degree angle waiting to make his run, when Dalglish slips the ball through the Everton cover into open space, and Rush is suddenly like a lurcher let off the leash. He gets in his first shot, left-footed, under challenge, and the ball beats Neville Southall but hits the post. Before the goalkeeper or his defence can react, Rush has pounced on the rebound and angled the ball home.

For his fourth and final goal of the day, Rush simply latches onto Sammy Lee's through ball, sprints towards the Everton goal and takes it round Southall at pace before turning it home with his right foot. And this against the team he grew up supporting as a kid. What, I wonder, might Rush have done if he *hadn't* liked Everton?

'My first ever goal against Everton was a deflection off my shoulder,' he remembers, 'and so for some reason they were always a lucky team for me to play against. I think their defence probably played the offside trap too much, which was ideal for me and Kenny.'

Bob Paisley must have been able to retire with an easy conscience that season, with his team in good order and the youngsters he'd developed making such headlines. Paisley got the Manager of the Year award in 1983, Dalglish the Player of the Year and Rush the Young Player of the Year award.

With a new manager taking over for the next season, albeit Joe Fagan who was promoted from within, there was always a slim chance that Liverpool might have relaxed for a season, looked at their haul of trophies, basked in glory, started believing in their own publicity, and gone on the piss in a big way. Some chance.

For Rush in particular, 1983–84 turned into the mother of all seasons. He scored 32 goals in 41 league games, scoring in 22 of those matches. In the home game against Luton Town, he struck five as Liverpool won 6–0. David Pleat, the Luton manager, sportingly declared afterwards that 'it was painful to watch, but beautiful'.

Rush also scored a superb hat-trick at Aston Villa in a freezing cold midweek match in January. His first was a low right-footer on the run, slotted home from the edge of the area, his second a crashing left-foot volley from 18 yards, and his third a remarkably delicate chip after he had controlled the ball on his thigh. He later scored four in a 5–0 home win over Coventy at the end of the season. But Rush was no less potent in the League Cup, scoring eight on the road to Wembley, but none in the final even though Everton were the opposition. 'I was getting great service from Souness and Dalglish and I'd also learned to concentrate more. And I knew that, with Liverpool, if you missed one chance another would be along pretty soon.'

It was in the European Cup, however, that Rush showed that he was now an international class striker, not just some bully of duff domestic teams. His spring-heeled header in Bilbao put Athletic out, and then he got one in each leg against Benfica. But it was in the cauldron of the away leg against Dinamo Bucharest that Rush stood tallest. The violent atmosphere around the ground seemed to be the classic recipe for a cup upset abroad, strange faces, an ugly, depressing place, muscular opponents not overly bothered about where they kicked you. Well, Rushie did for the Romanians, turning past two defenders to strike a great left-foot shot into the far corner to 'kill off the crowd', as he puts it, after just 12 minutes, and then finishing the job with another smartly taken goal six minutes from time, to smother any last frantic rallies by the home side. The whole team showed incredible courage in that game, and an iron resolve to win.

After that, Roma in the final must have seemed like a friendly, and Liverpool played like it for a large part of the time, controlling the game with relaxed, rhythmic passing. When it came to the penalty shoot-out Rush was one of the brave ones to step up and score, making up for all the disappointment of Paris three years earlier. He scored 47 goals in all for Liverpool that season – not counting the Roma penalty – and also got two goals for Wales. He won the Golden Boot as Europe's leading scorer, and was named Footballer of the Year by both the PFA and the Football Writers Association. If he'd had any sense, he would have retired then . . . though, in fact, Rush's proposed move to Napoli was blocked by the Liverpool chairman, John Smith.

The 1984–85 season was overshadowed by Heysel, but Rush was also injured for a while, missing 14 league games. Liverpool surrendered the Championship to Everton and the League Cup to Norwich, after being knocked out by Tottenham. But it was a season to forget in every respect.

But 1985–86, with his partner Dalglish now player-manager, was another memorable one for Rush. Twenty goals in 40 league games, and then his wonderful, icy goalscoring in the Cup final against Everton, after the Blues had taken a 1–0 lead into the interval. His first was a masterpiece of timing in his run onto a shrewd Molby pass; his second a ruthless act of instant control and powerful finishing from Ronnie Whelan's chipped pass. 'It was a great day for me,' he says. 'My first Cup final *and* playing Everton all rolled into one. It still stands out in my memory.'

In the circumstances of winning the Double with Liverpool, it was hardly surprising that Rush, with all his goals, should have become a target for European sides. Juventus, of all clubs, came in for him, and although they initially wanted him immediately, a late change of mind by Michel Platini meant that the Turin club's foreign quotient was complete for that season. The deal stood, but Rush would have another season with Liverpool before the move. To the fans it seemed a messy compromise, but most were simply grateful that we hadn't lost him yet, especially as Dalglish had announced his decision to play fewer and fewer games.

Although Liverpool had a blank season as far as trophies were concerned, Rush left the Kop with some sparkling memories as he played in every league game, scoring 30 goals, with a further ten in the two domestic cup competitions. In the last home game against Watford, he scored what we believed would be his final goal for Liverpool, before donating his kit to the Kop. It was *arrivederci* Rushie, and hello, Aldo, Beardo and Barnesie.

Although Rush's single year at Juventus is down as a failure, it should be said in mitigation that he was joining a team fading from great heights. Platini had gone, leaving little creative juice in the midfield. Rush, as ever, did his best, and didn't deserve some of the music-hall-style routines which were spread about him – about the baked beans, and the tea-bags and all that English-misfit-abroad stuff. 'I was a bit unlucky that Platini didn't carry on playing. But I still scored 14 goals and I learned an awful lot about life and people. I was certainly a better player for being out in Italy.'

But by the time he came back to Liverpool, a new team had been formed and it was almost as though he was no longer compatible with this new body. 'Not to be unkind to the guy, but Rush was never the same player once Kenny stopped playing,' Graeme Souness says. He was also unfortunate that his first season back embraced the trauma of Hillsborough. Liverpool, not just the team but the city itself, lost a great deal of willpower after that. Rush still went on as substitute in the FA Cup final against Everton, and scored two of the goals in our 3–2 victory. And he improved as soon as John Aldridge moved on, as he helped Liverpool take their last title in 1990. But when Dalglish left as manager, Rush assumed a new role, as senior professional, under Graeme Souness, eventually becoming captain. He also got another Cup final goal against Sunderland in 1992.

I think time will show that he did a lot of good work on Robbie Fowler in those comparatively barren years of the 1990s. It may be that, as Ray Clemence observed, Rush hung on too late to make a move to a winning club, but that was because he cared for Liverpool so much. 'I just loved playing for Liverpool and the fans. It was as simple as that, really.' After his frustrating year with Leeds, it's good that Rushie has been reunited with Dalglish at Newcastle, giving him the chance of a competitive farewell to the game rather than a lingering loss of form and a slow drift down the divisions. Even if that had happened, I can't imagine anyone ever coming up to him with the classic put-down of old footballers: 'Didn't you used to be Ian Rush?' Because, to us, he will always be Ian Rush.

JOHN BARNES

Move On Up

It was the morning after Liverpool had lost disastrously, 3–0, to Paris St Germain in the first leg of the European Cup-Winners' Cup semi-final last April. The game, shown live on terrestrial television, had been a prime-time display of all the things that had been cited as wrong with the modern Liverpool team. Depending on who you listened to, 'they had no heart', 'they were too busy modelling clothes to worry about football', 'it doesn't hurt them anymore when they lose', 'they're playing the wrong system', 'all they can do is pass for passing's sake'.

These aren't the comments of the people I shared a Liverpool bar with while watching the game – although I heard much the same thing – but of some of the former professional Liverpool footballers featured in this book. And these remarks were all made *before* that débâcle in Paris.

So Melwood didn't strike me as a particularly comfortable place to be that morning, less than eight or so hours since the players touched down at Speke Airport, less than two hours since they saw the back pages – if they looked at them at all, that is. First-team training was back under way in a distant corner of the Melwood complex, and you could hear the usual shouts and laughs and banter drifting across on the wind. So you guess one of two things – that the spirit of players is remarkably resilient even in the face of an embarrassing defeat; or, that they don't give a toss, etcetera, etcetera. Only they will know, I suppose.

Phil Babb passes the waiting press pack with a resigned grin: 'Be after a few scalps this morning, eh, lads?' Nobody says anything. An hour later, after the players have had a clear-the-air team meeting with manager Roy Evans, the Liverpool captain, John Barnes, appears and looks for my face. Despite the apparent trauma of the previous evening, he's happy to talk, and to defend his team.

Dressed in a relatively sober (for him), all-white tracksuit with huge DKNY lettering across the chest, he escorts me into the gymnasium and relaxes on a bench. 'It was a good meeting,' he says, without any hint of spin-doctoring. But what Barnes couldn't know was that, nearly a decade after he had joined Liverpool, the countdown had already started on the ending of his career at the club. This doesn't invalidate his words in this book, because they were concentrated primarily on what he had achieved already. But it does add a poignancy to those passages where he addressed both his own and the club's future, and which I have left intact. Nor have I attempted, other than in this paragraph, to be wise after the event. Neither Barnes nor I knew what was coming, although the volume of cheering which greeted his substitution in the home game against Manchester United, just a week after our interview, had all of us in the press-box feeling a sudden chill in the air.

Barnes wasn't picked for the return leg against Paris, and those who wanted him out would have pointed to the team's much-improved performance in winning 2–0, using the old flat back-four system, and getting the ball forward much more quickly than had been the case for most of the season. But though the exclusion of Barnes continued, Liverpool's form soon reverted to its recent stereotype – a patchy home win over Spurs, a 2–1 defeat at Wimbledon which finally erased any mathematical possibility of winning the Premiership, and then the dismal draw at Sheffield Wednesday which allowed Newcastle United to finish second and a claim a place in the Champions' League.

Although Barnes played in several of Liverpool's pre-season friendlies in the summer, and was allocated his usual number 10 shirt in the official squad line-up, the arrival in the close-season of a clutch of midfield players – Oyvind Leonhardsen from Wimbledon, Danny Murphy from Crewe and Paul Ince from Inter Milan – suggested that there would be no way back. After the first game of the season, at Wimbledon, when Murphy had been called from the bench as a substitute rather than Barnes, Roy Evans announced that Liverpool had granted the player a free transfer.

Within a week, the man who had brought Barnes to Anfield, Kenny Dalglish, had taken him to Newcastle. Dalglish is no sentimentalist, so taking Barnes was as pragmatic a gesture as taking on Ian Rush in the same fashion. Neither move would have happened had Alan Shearer not been so traumatically injured. But Dalglish knows their ways, they know his, so no big explanations are required. Though Barnes expressed 'some sadness' at leaving Anfield, we can often exaggerate footballers' sensitivities. They deal with intense emotions on an almost daily basis, so they become practised at dealing with them and with sudden turns in personal fortune. What Barnes and Rush both showed was a self-belief that they still had something to offer at the highest level – whether this is self-delusion, only time will tell.

So this chapter becomes not just a celebration of what Barnes gave to Liverpool Football Club and its fans for ten seasons, but also an assessment of what he achieved. In the first instance, let me say that I think Barnes is among an élite group of half a dozen or so players who not only contributed their football skills to Liverpool, but whose demeanour also added to the general prestige of the club as an internationally known institution. It used to be the case, when I first travelled abroad in 1966, that you simply had to say 'Bobby Charlton' in order to establish your Englishness and strike up a conversation, in the common language of football, with a local citizen. Today, I think I could get by in most continental bars by mentioning Barnes, Dalglish, Rush, Souness, Keegan, Robbie Fowler, and perhaps Steve McManaman if I was in Barcelona. Three of those names have played abroad with various levels of success, while Souness now manages in Italy. Barnes has done neither – unless you take his native Jamaican status literally and say that England was his foreign country. But his brilliant footballing skills took the game up to another level, like all great players do, and his cool and articulate persona has also made him what the agents call a 'marquee name'.

Of course the wonderful goal he scored for England against Brazil in the Maracana Stadium in 1984 must have inspired generations of kids around the world, just as Cruyff did with his turn against that East German full-back in the 1974 World Cup, or when Pele nearly scored from the halfway line against the Czechs four years earlier in Mexico, or even when Maradona scored his second, legitimate goal against England in 1986. These moments extend the boundaries of what can be achieved on a football pitch, and encourage those that follow to go one better.

On a domestic level, Barnes transformed the general perception of Liverpool as a wonderfully efficient team into one of extraordinary flamboyance, particularly during his first three seasons between 1987 and 1990. Just as importantly, perhaps more so, his presence as a black footballer in a city not noted for its tradition of racial tolerance helped reshape outmoded notions and behaviour. His has been, by any standards, a remarkable journey.

Born into an upper-class Jamaican family, with a sporting bent, Barnes says, 'I played football all the time as a kid, even though there were no professional leagues or clubs on the island. But my dad played football for Jamaica, and I also swam a great deal because my sister was an international swimmer.'

He grew up watching English football on the *Star Soccer* television programme, and remembers being excited by the broadcasts of the 1974 World Cup. 'I think I must have been the only kid in Jamaica who supported Germany in the final against Holland. In fact, I remember crying when Holland got a penalty in the first minute. The Germans were my favourites, partly because my dad had been to the 1972 Olympics in Munich and brought me back a pair of Gerd Muller Adidas football boots. The Germans also had Wolfgang Overath, a wonderful left-sided midfield player, who I modelled myself on at that time.' The fact that Barnes always claimed the number 10 shirt at Liverpool may have less to do with its South American mystique as the shirt worn by Pele, Zico and Maradona among others, and more to do with Overath wearing the same number for West Germany.

Barnes came to England as a 13-year-old, when his father, a colonel in the Jamaican Army, became the military attaché at the

London embassy. He played football at his grammar school, and with a boys club, before joining the amateur side Sudbury Court, where he often played as a centre-half. It was while he was playing for Sudbury that a local Watford fan – 'I think he was a taxi driver,' says Barnes – tipped off Bertie Mee, the club's general manager, who had Barnes professionally 'scouted' and then watched himself before offering him the chance to train with the Watford youth team. 'I had no idea anybody had been watching me at all,' Barnes recalls. 'The first I knew about it was when Bertie Mee made contact.' Within months he was offered a professional contract, and when his family returned to Jamaica, he stayed on in England to pursue a career in football.

There was always something indefinable about John Barnes from the moment he started playing for Watford's first team in the early 1980s. They deployed him as a left-winger, supplying crosses for their beanpole centre-forward Ross Jenkins. Yet he was always more than that. At that time, when I wasn't watching Liverpool, I used to go to the odd game with Richard Williams, an old friend from *Time Out* days, who was a Nottingham Forest supporter. The rationale in going to these 'foreign' matches was simply to find something entertaining at clubs we wouldn't normally bother watching. Because of Barnes, we were frequent visitors to Vicarage Road, waiting for him to produce something exotic. We were rarely disappointed. The young Barnes possessed the skill and the movement of the best Brazilians – he would do drag-backs with the sole of his left boot; he would nutmeg defenders; he would do un-English things like dribble the ball; and he could bend his free-kicks like Garrincha. And all this in the utilitarian team that Graham Taylor had fashioned.

But at least Taylor picked him and didn't try to change him. When it came to playing for England, Barnes seemed to be constantly messed around by Bobby Robson. In for one game, out for the next. He seemed to be following orders to stick to the touchline, to let the left-back Kenny Sansom go on the overlap past him and get the crosses in. In the early stages it seemed that he and another black winger, Mark Chamberlain of Stoke City, were interchangeable in the manager's mind. After Rio, Barnes did get some kind of run, but when it came to the 1986 World Cup, his only appearance was as a substitute against Argentina, coming on when England were 2–0 down. He made one goal, taking on two defenders and crossing from the left for Gary Lineker to head home. He very nearly created another as he danced past the Argentine cover again to curl in a cross which beat the goalkeeper and needed a desperate goal-line clearance to stop Lineker scoring again. It was one of those performances when you wonder what might have happened had he been on from the start.

With Watford's form now waning, Barnes looked too good a player to be forgotten. Yet after the 1986 World Cup and his small but dazzling contribution, nobody came in for him. I suspect that it was part of the same thinking which seemed to make Bobby Robson so suspicious of his talent. In ruthless, professional terms, Barnes was probably regarded as a 'luxury player', nice to have when things are going well, but a liability when they're not. The Puritan thinking which has always been at the core of English football philosophy – until very recently, that is – had becalmed many other careers, irrespective of race. A rough list of exciting mavericks who were allowed to light up the English game for brief periods would include Frank Worthington (whom Shankly tried to sign in 1971 before hearing about his exotic private life), Stan Bowles, Duncan McKenzie, Tony Currie, Alan Hudson and Laurie Cunningham. By the end of 1987, it looked as if John Barnes might become one of them.

Although he was known to be available for transfer, nobody came for him. Not Spurs, not Arsenal for whom he was alleged to have been waiting. And, Barnes says, 'There were one or two whispers about Monaco but nothing concrete,' refuting some suspicions on Merseyside that he only came to Liverpool as a second choice, once a move abroad had broken down. 'Liverpool was a very happy choice, I promise you. It went wonderfully well from day one. The first time I played was in a pre-season friendly in Germany against Bayern Munich; we lost 3–2 but I scored and I could see instantly how things would develop, and that we would take some stopping.

Our first three league games were away from home, because the Kop was closed to repair a sewer, so I had a chance to dispel some of that scepticism which might have been there, without the pressure of performing at Anfield.'

Liverpool won 2–1 at Arsenal on the opening day as they paraded their new front line of Barnes, Peter Beardsley and John Aldridge, who had been brought in earlier that year once the news of Ian Rush's transfer to Juventus had broken. Barnes provided the precise cross from the left which Aldridge headed home for the first goal. At Coventry they won 4–1, with Aldridge and Beardsley each getting a goal, and then they drew at West Ham, before finally entertaining Oxford at Anfield on 12 September. The word about Barnes 'on the road' had already been good, but that afternoon the Kop had it confirmed for their own eyes. He was calm and masterful, in control of the ball at all times, provided a cross to Aldridge for the first goal and then, to top it all, he scored a wonderful goal from a free-kick, curling the ball around the Oxford defensive wall, after he himself had been fouled. A new chant was added to the Kop's repertoire, to the speeded-up tune of 'Here We Go', they chanted, 'Johnny Barnes, Johnny Barnes, Johnny Barnes!' as though he had been a Liverpool player all his life.

'It just gelled instantly with me, Peter [Beardsley] and John [Aldridge]. Although I'd been an out-and-out winger with Watford, Liverpool let me play more in a Ray Kennedy role. It was a position where I could help create things, and help defensively, and still get wide if the opportunity arose. It was very important for my development as a player. My evolution within the team was linked to the way the team played. Being at Liverpool added a whole new dimension to my game, and my awareness and appreciation of the team's movement improved enormously. At Watford I was just "up and down", taking on people so I could get a cross in, coming inside occasionally to score goals. But at Liverpool I was allowed much more freedom of movement. And that team was just wonderful to play in. I thought we'd win the Double every year.'

Liverpool did their best to fulfil Barnes's predictions that season. Their buoyant form saw them go undefeated in the league for the first 29 games, as Aldridge, Beardsley and Barnes all reached double-figure totals for goals. One of John's two goals at home to QPR was a virtuoso solo effort, as he intercepted a pass near the halfway line, then swerved through the QPR defence before curling a shot high past David Seaman.

By the turn of the year, Liverpool had scored four goals in a match on eight occasions. It wasn't until mid-March that, with Leeds United's record start to a season now equalled by Liverpool and about to be beaten, Everton did their usual spoiling job by winning the return derby match at Goodison 1–0. Liverpool lost only one more league game, 2–1 away at Forest in April, and finished with a set of figures that matched the performance of the 1978–79 team:

played	40
won	26
drew	12
lost	2
for	87
against	24
points	90

Liverpool finished nine points clear of Manchester United, with a goal difference of +63!

The only cloud in this otherwise golden sky had come in the first match against Everton at Anfield in November. Nothing to do with the result – Liverpool won easily 2–0 – but at one point when Barnes was taking a corner at the Anfield Road End, where the Everton fans were housed, a handful of bananas were thrown from the crowd and scattered around Barnes's feet. Apart from back-heeling a couple of them into touch, as a player would with any detritus on the pitch, Barnes showed no reaction to this racial insult, although plenty of Liverpool fans, a touch sanctimoniously, did, shaking their fists at Everton's supporters and phoning the club afterwards to complain.

Amid the storm, Barnes remained calm and silent. To some critics he was being too passive in the face of a vile insult and he was duty-bound to react. To others, myself included, his dignified silence was an apt response to a contemptible but otherwise non-life-threatening gesture by a few disordered fans. Yes, it would have been good if the morons who did it had been caught on camera, or nabbed by the police on duty, or even shopped by the fans around them, but the one consolation was that, as far as I'm aware, it didn't happen to Barnes again.

This is where Barnes made his impact on Liverpool, the city. Both sets of supporters had always celebrated a casual racism, as opposed to organised, from the very first days when I started going to matches. In the mid 1960s, the Kop used to chant 'Coco Pops!' at Leeds United's South African township winger Albert Johansen. When Bermuda's Clyde Best appeared for West Ham he would often be greeted by a chorus of the 'Banana Boat Song' – 'Day-oh, day-ay-ay-oh!' or, more ploddingly, a chant of 'Hello der man! Hello der man!' in a cod attempt at a Caribbean accent. And in the late '70s and early '80s, as the second wave of black players – most of them *born* in England – came into the game, the monkey noises became an increasingly familiar sound. And this despite Liverpool having some of the oldest African and Chinese communities in Britain.

There were few black faces on the Kop, even fewer in the city centre when I used to go to the Mardi Gras club in Mount Pleasant in the late 1960s, or to the Odd Spot in Bold Street. Only at The Sink, on Hardman Street, which bordered the Upper Parliament Street area, did the races mix in a shared celebration of the music of Tamla Motown and Stax. Otherwise the city was a no-go area for black youths, even though they spoke with Scouse accents, as their fathers and grandfathers had.

And as far as I can remember, only Cliff Marshall at Everton and Howard Gayle at Liverpool ever made a brief breakthrough into the first-team squads before Barnes arrived on Merseyside. Gayle made only three full appearances and two as substitute while he was at Liverpool. Ten years on from when Barnes joined the club, the 1997–98 team photo showed no fewer than six black faces in the squad. But there is more work to be done to encourage supporters and players from Afro-Caribbean backgrounds to be a part of the Liverpool set-up – only reserve goalkeeper Tony Warner is a local lad. But the influence of John Barnes is there for all to see. Racist chanting or sloganeering is a thing of the past at Anfield, and though it may have begun on a simplistic 'well, I wouldn't do that to Johnny Barnes, so why should I do it to one of their players' basis, the banality of racism seems to have sunk in. Barnes has, in addition, made dozens of appearances at Football Trust meetings promoting the anti-racism message in the game. His legacy to the club in this area is a valuable and, I would guess, a lasting one.

While a few bananas took the edge off 1988, Wimbledon also helped Liverpool slip up at Wembley, where Dennis Wise was deployed to shadow Barnes. Aldridge's missed penalty and the referee disallowing Beardsley's goal didn't help the cause either. One Double just missed.

'The team had the best of all elements. Individualists, plus the hard work of Ray Houghton on the right, and Steve McMahon and Ronnie Whelan in the middle. Just an excellent team. Kenny used to keep us fresh with the five-a-sides, in which he often played, but we were a bunch of players who were inspired by each other out on the pitch. We were playing almost telepathically at times.'

One such occasion was the game against Nottingham Forest on 13 April, when Liverpool attacked with outstanding fluency to beat a very good side 5–0. I can remember Barnes setting up one goal by chasing a ball to the left touchline, keeping it in with the sole of his foot, turning, nutmegging a Forest defender and then crossing into the six-yard box for Aldridge to pop in the goal. It was a night the great Tom Finney, no mean attacking winger in his own time, described as 'the finest ever performance by an English club side'. So there. Barnes won the Footballer of the Year award for the first time, after just one season with Liverpool.

The 1988–89 season was, as we know, blighted by Hillsborough. Barnes was prominent among the players at the many funerals, enhancing the affection which the fans were developing for him. For the record, Liverpool missed another Double by the fraction of Arsenal's superior goalscoring, having finished equal on points and on goal difference, after their dramatic 2–0 win at Anfield. Liverpool again beat Everton in the FA Cup final, 3–2 in extra-time, with Barnes supplying the cross for Rush's second, the winning goal.

In among all the sorrows was a professional one for Barnes – the realisation that a team this good could have made a great impact on Europe had the Heysel ban not been in force. 'It was a sadness – that's the right word – rather than a regret, because there wasn't anything I could do about it. By the time we got back into Europe, that side had dissolved and, with a whole lot of youngsters coming through, we didn't do Liverpool credit.'

In the 1989–90 season, however, Barnes himself was absolutely unstoppable. 'Completely frightening,' recalls his captain, Alan Hansen. 'I don't think I've seen one individual put in a season like it. It was entertainment plus.' Barnes scored 28 goals in all competitions – two more than Ian Rush, who says of that season: 'Barnes was just irresistible, and scored some truly spectacular goals.'

This was the year that Crystal Palace were beaten 9–0 at Anfield; Chelsea lost 5–1; Swansea were hammered 8–0 in the FA Cup; and Coventry were beaten 6–1 in front of their own fans, with Barnes getting his first hat-trick, on the last day of the season. Liverpool were champions for the 18th time, nine points clear of nearest challengers Aston Villa. But, yet again, a potential Double was tossed away in the bizarre circumstances of the 3–4 defeat to Crystal Palace in the FA Cup semi-final. Barnes was voted Footballer of the Year for the second time in three seasons, and joined the likes of Stanley Matthews, Tom Finney, Danny Blanchflower and Kenny Dalglish in the exclusive club of two-time winners.

'By then Liverpool had more or less perfected the ability to play in units. And then link it all up through the midfielders to the front men. We were able to translate the discipline and skills of five-a-side on a small pitch to the 11-a-side game on a big pitch. But there were no tactics in that team – we just knew how to play, knew each other's strengths. It just worked out.'

Though the nucleus of that team went into the 1990–91 season, it couldn't have known that Liverpool had won their last Championship for a long while. Some of the first signs of decay were there to see, but nobody wanted to believe them. Nobody wanted to believe that Dalglish had resigned as manager either, or that Alan Hansen was finally retiring. The famous 4–4 draw at Goodison Park in the FA Cup in February 1991 – 'a great game of football', insists Barnes – became a swan-song for the Liverpool era of dominance, as it also, in turn, became the catalyst for Dalglish's resignation. Both Barnes and Beardsley scored cherishable goals that night, but they now seem like floral tributes at a memorial service.

'As players left after Kenny's resignation, and some of the youngsters had to be brought in, I knew that it would be difficult for three or four years, that we'd be pushing for fourth or fifth place in the Championship rather than winning it. I personally believe that Graeme Souness let too many older players go too soon, before they'd had the chance to pass on their experience to the likes of McManaman, Redknapp and Fowler. The change was too rapid. What Liverpool had always done was bought good players too, experienced players. But they didn't do that in 1991 and 1992, they just let a lot of youngsters come through the ranks. It was maybe a bit early for some of them at the time. For the others, we'll probably see the benefits soon, because there are a lot of young players here with a great deal of experience behind them. This team will improve. I think the level of individual talent in the side is as high as any Liverpool team in the past – maybe higher.'

It should be noted here that not once during the seven seasons since the last Championship was there a mention of Barnes leaving. On a purely selfish level, he should probably have got out – gone to Italy while he was still at his peak. But he chose to stay at Liverpool, taking on the role of captain in a side that had stopped winning trophies on a regular basis, which seems almost heroic to me. 'I've always been a talker and a thinker on the pitch,' Barnes says, 'so it was a natural progression for me to make. If you watch me on the pitch I'm always talking, cajoling, sometimes ranting, even!'

He also defends the current squad against all charges, made by former players as well as the fans, that they have somehow lost the Liverpool tradition of toughing it out when the circumstances aren't right. 'You have to remember that with all this money coming into the game, every club has more resources available. It's not a case of the big boys getting worse, but everyone else getting better. It's terribly competitive. But as far as the players are concerned, I can promise you they still hurt, though some show it more than others. Football's got a wider social horizon now, and it's not a bad thing for young players to have more to do. All those older players, who go on about the young lacking pride and passion compared to when they were picking up £100 per week, have got it wrong. Maybe we can switch off quicker than the older players used to, but that doesn't mean we haven't got pride. The world is getting better! The world is a more comfortable place and we shouldn't be ashamed of that, and we shouldn't have to answer to the players of the past going on about "when I was a lad". You should just say, "Well, unlucky, you should have been born now!" That's the way the world is, unfortunately, and if you're old, unlucky!'

Whatever John Barnes achieves at Newcastle, it seems likely – no, make that *certain* – that a movement into management awaits him: 'It appeals to me and I think I've got a lot to offer.' He's inspired by what Ruud Gullit and Glenn Hoddle have been able to do in redefining the role of the modern, progressive coach, and he has already made a trip to Ajax Amsterdam's academy to see how it all works. He won't plan for anything, though, because he knows just how unpredictable the game is.

So we shouldn't see his leaving Anfield, sad though it was, as an end, either for him or for Liverpool. While it is tempting to say that Liverpool will never see his like again, that draws a line under the club's potential and under those who might follow him in the red jersey, whether they're from Liverpool or Outer Mongolia. John Barnes, above all others, has shown there are no limits to skill and imagination where football is concerned.

Duggie's Doin's

When they laid Bob Paisley to rest after his death on 14 February 1996, it brought to a close a remarkable life by any standards, not just football's. At the time, it was tempting to think that a last link with the old order of the game had gone to the grave with him. Certainly his 44 years of active service for Liverpool – more if you include his directorship and his advisory role when Kenny Dalglish was manager – is unlikely to be surpassed in these days when a contract between a manager and the football club's plc board that employs him is mutually regarded as a readily disposable item.

Then there is the question of Paisley's lineage. Like the other great managers with whom he can now be confidently numbered – Jock Stein, Matt Busby, and his celebrated predecessor at Liverpool, Bill Shankly – Paisley had the sort of background where football offered an almost magical release from the industrial drudgery of the coal pit, the factory or, in his case, as an apprentice bricklayer in the building trade in County Durham. None of these great men – and the adjective is meant to embrace qualities beyond their football achievements – ever forgot the apparent blessing bestowed upon them, whereby they were suddenly being paid for doing something they loved, especially after a war had intervened to remind them all of their mortality.

Today, the modern player arrives in the game sensing the infinite horizons ahead of him, aware of the opportunities to get rich. He is tooled up with agents, accountants and contracts with fashion houses and boot manufacturers, and mostly convinced of the view that everything he gets out of the game he'll deserve, irrespective of what he achieves on the pitch. And he'll see it as the product of merit rather than luck.

For men like Paisley, however, a simple involvement with football was in itself a precious gift, not to be squandered. Football was both a triviality when compared to war and industrial drudgery, but also something precious because it had given meaning to so many lives, not just those who were fortunate to play it, but also those who watched from the terraces after Saturday-morning shifts at the docks or the factory.

This attitude, translated into management, helped Paisley drive his team on to produce the astonishing run of success – six Championships, three European Cups, one UEFA Cup and three League Cups – which he achieved in his nine seasons in charge of Liverpool. And here I've discounted a few minor baubles like the Charity Shield and the European Super Cup.

Yet it would do Paisley a disservice to try to define him as the last true football man, with its connotations of centre-partings, boot-room camaraderie and home-spun values, because although he embraced all of these, he was also one of the great thinkers and modernisers of the English game. This paradox was enshrined within his appearance and demeanour. When, as a fledgling feature writer with London's listing magazine *Time Out*, I first proposed an interview with him early in 1977, Paisley's understandably cautious approach to the media after the wild, epigrammatic days of Shanks, was only laid aside because my dad had happened to be a Saturday settler in a betting shop where Paisley often adjourned to relax. The very idea of Paisley and a trendy magazine like *Time Out* coming together seemed to be a joke, but the interview I had with him in February 1977, and a subsequent one before the 1978 European Cup, proved to be remarkably candid and lucid for a man who was pretty canny at presenting himself as an innocent duffer to the press.

When I met Paisley for the first talk, in the hessian wallpapered players' lounge at Anfield, I assumed that his appearance – brown zip-up cardigan with leather patch-pockets, and carpet slippers – was a reflection of our informal connection, there being no need to dress up for the son of somebody who works in a bookie's. But, 15 months later, virtually the same wardrobe appeared again, such was Paisley's projected self-image. I say 'projected' here, because I think that he liked to take the pressure off himself by being portrayed as a kindly, avuncular type rather than some gold-clad Pharoah like Ron Atkinson. It didn't mean he was any less ambitious than these other, flashier managers, but I suspect he'd worked out that while their suits and jewels might buy them some good publicity in the beginning, they were the first source of ridicule when the going got tough.

The quiet, hesitant Geordie voice completed the 'favourite uncle' package, but it was the clinical authority of Paisley's words which confirmed that here was a man who knew much more about football than his natural modesty would let him admit. His low-key acceptance of Shankly's legacy ('I asked the players about it and they were for me having a go, and I thought, well, a new man wouldn't know our routines, and that was that . . .') was plainly designed to buy himself some time, but there was no doubt about his appetite for the job, or his iron desire to make a success of it.

Paisley had been born in Hetton-le-Hole, Durham, and though he'd spent a year working on open-cast mining, it was as a bricklayer that he seemed destined to spend his working life. But playing football, for perhaps the most famous amateur side in the game, Bishop Auckland, brought him to Liverpool's attention in 1939, and he signed for the club that May as a 19-year-old half-back for a wage of £5 per week, and a joining fee of £10. He was allowed to complete his season with Bishop Auckland by playing in the Amateur Cup final, at Sunderland, in which they beat Willington 3–0 after extra-time.

Paisley joined a Liverpool team who had just finished a mediocre 11th in the First Division, and among the playing staff was a Scottish wing-half named Matt Busby. The start of the Second World War in September 1939 saw the Football League immediately abandoned after just three matches, but regional games were staged from October onwards to keep up the nation's morale. Paisley played in two short seasons of these matches before army duty took him out to Egypt in August 1941; he spent nearly four years in the desert campaign before switching to Italy. When, in May 1977, before Liverpool's first European Cup final, he was asked by the Italian football press if he had been to Rome before, he was able to quip, 'Aye, the last time I was here I helped liberate it!'

The Football League resumed properly in season 1946–47, with Liverpool eventually becoming the first post-war champions. The team then included the likes of Cyril Sidlow in goal, Albert Stubbins at centre-forward, Bob Paisley at left-half and Billy Liddell on the left wing. Busby, offered the job of managing the new Liverpool, had preferred to revive Manchester United . . .

Liverpool reached the semi-final of the FA Cup that year, but lost to Burnley, setting in train a long sequence of bad luck where Paisley and the FA Cup were concerned. In 1950, he scored one of the goals against Everton which put Liverpool into the final, but found himself out of the team on the great day itself, despite the fact that his name was already printed in the team's line-up for the Wembley programme.

In virtually every interview he gave, Paisley made reference to this incident, not just to reveal the hurt it had caused him, but also the decisiveness it gave him when it came to dropping somebody for a big game: 'It was probably the biggest disappointment of my life, but it stood me in good stead as a manager, for whenever I left someone out I could say, "I know how you feel, son," and he'd know that I meant it.'

The incident may also have generated another line in Paisley's football philosophy, because he had missed the league match before Wembley with a knock, hoping to be 100 per cent on the day. But the lesson learnt was that you couldn't miss games and expect to get straight back into the side, and it was something scores of Liverpool players also learnt to their cost during their careers.

Paisley played four more seasons for Liverpool, once making the England B squad for a game in Holland, before retiring on a low note after Liverpool had finished bottom of the First Division in 1954 and been relegated. He was persuaded by the chairman, T.V. Williams, to forsake bricklaying and take a job on the coaching staff as the reserve-team manager – the reserves went on to win the Central League title in the third year of his stewardship. But Liverpool's first team was still in the Second Division, and as a succession of managers failed to lift them back, the former Scotland international Bill Shankly was brought in as team manager from Huddersfield in December 1959.

Paisley's Liverpool career could have ended there and then. These days, new managers invariably clear out the existing coaching staff and bring in their own crew. But Shankly kept on most of the back-room staff, though he did go through the playing staff like a dose of salts as he sought to turn Liverpool's fortunes around.

We've heard from Chris Lawler, Tommy Smith and Peter Thompson how Shankly rebuilt Liverpool – the team, the club and the ground. But Paisley's role – as reserve-team coach, physiotherapist and then first-team trainer – was also vital in the process. It wasn't a case of Mozart and Salieri, with a jealous rival scheming against his more talented colleague. This was one of the truly great partnerships in football. Together they formed a formidable pairing, Shankly with his drive and motivational skills, Bob with his knowledge of tactics, injuries and player psychology. They worked the 'good cop/bad cop routine' to perfection on players they thought were malingering or lacking confidence. Chris Lawler says that he 'found Bob much easier to deal with than Shanks, because he listened to your problems. Shanks would just ignore you. After I'd got married the day before the Inter Milan game, Shankly still wanted me to go on the players' trip to Majorca, without wives, despite the fact that I'd had no honeymoon. We had a big argument about it for over half an hour, and he just wouldn't give in. I think Paisley would have been more understanding.'

And as we've heard from Smith and Thompson, Shankly could go instantly cold on players once they had appeared to have outlived their usefulness to the team. Paisley was as hard and ruthless in his own way, but his decisions would be taken for the benefit of the team, not on the suspicion of human obsolescence.

In terms of football, I've heard from several sources that Paisley was probably the shrewder judge of a player's ability, and what position would bring the best out of him. When Liverpool signed Alec Lindsay from Bury in 1969, for example, Shankly saw him staying in his left-half role, despite his lack of pace. One First

Division coach, who shared tea in the Liverpool boot-room after a match around that time, told me that 'it was Bob's idea to move Lindsay to full-back where his passing could be exploited, and his lack of pace protected. I know, because I was there when he suggested it!'

Similarly, when Shankly left Liverpool in 1974, bequeathing Arsenal forward Ray Kennedy to Paisley, it proved at first to be a fairly duff inheritance, with the previously free-scoring Kennedy getting only five goals in the 23 games he played in his first season. Once Paisley had converted Kennedy to a left-sided midfield player, however, it all changed, and Kennedy became one of the most effective passers, runners and scorers in the game, wearing the number 5 shirt.

Paisley's succession to the Shankly job is shrouded a little in mystery. It is said that Shankly told the board he was the man for the job, but boardroom sources say it was their idea. No matter, really, for what counted was the players' acceptance of their new boss, and his willingness to take the job on. 'When the board asked me to move up to manager, I had to have a think about it,' Paisley told me.

Ray Clemence remembers the mood in the dressing-room when the news of the upheaval broke: 'We were all stunned when Shanks left, because nobody had seen it coming. When Bob came into the dressing-room on the first day of pre-season training, he basically apologised that Bill had left the club, and said that though he himself hadn't really wanted the job, he'd been assigned to do it. All of us senior players looked at each other and thought, well, we've known Bob for a long time, we know he can't be another Shanks, but let's get behind him and give him all the help we can. And the best thing he did was to vow not to change anything, because it was sheer common sense not to. Everything was working, and the theories and philosophies would carry on. For me, Shanks was a fantastic motivator, and everything was about simplicity. Bob kept things simple too, but he was a very good tactician as well. He was very good at working out what a team's strengths and weaknesses were. His delivery of those ideas wasn't the best, but because he had experienced players around him, they knew what he was trying to get across. And everyone respected him for the way he went about the job, and everybody was behind him, so it welded us together even more.'

In one of the interviews I did with Paisley, he insisted, 'I did a lot of my best work in that first season in charge even though we only finished second. That was a failure by Liverpool standards. And it hurt me when a lot of the papers moaned that it wasn't the same now Bill had gone. You could almost feel some of them wanting me to hit the deck.'

But he also outlined the Liverpool philosophy as he now saw it, in charge, his own man. 'Our game is based on simple things. It's all about control and movement performed at pace, and about each player knowing his strengths and those of his team-mates. People think Liverpool are an over-coached side, but we're the least coached, least complicated side in the country. It's all about control of the ball – without that, you have no foundation for anything else. After that it's just a question of encouraging the players to think for themselves and each other. You don't see a Liverpool player give a ball and then stand still.'

A first Championship and a UEFA Cup in 1976 confirmed the validity of Paisley's ideas which, he freely acknowledged, had European football as one of its main sources. 'We don't go around with our eyes shut,' he told me. With an acute ability to find players able to fit into the system – Phil Neal, Jimmy Case, Joey Jones, Ray Kennedy and later Kenny Dalglish, Graeme Souness, Alan Hansen, and Mark Lawrenson – Paisley consolidated his first achievements, and very nearly took them to a historic treble in 1977. After that triumph in Rome he famously stayed sober so that he could relish every second of the night. And with the arrival of the 'Three Jocks' the following year, he had an engine-room that would drive the team throughout his remaining years as manager.

Despite the self-motivating qualities of his team, Paisley was still prone to playing his psychological games on some of the players if he thought they needed it to maintain their level of performance. 'We always try to play through a season at a high level,' he said. 'We don't want six-week merchants who have a good spell then disappear. Our lads come in after a good performance and they know they've got nothing owing to them. If anyone needs a reminder, I just take them on one side, ask him how the wife is, that sort of thing. He soon gets the message.'

One of the few players who didn't get this kind of treatment was Graeme Souness, the man Paisley made captain in the middle of the 1991–92 season. 'I had a special relationship with Bob,' Souness says, 'partly because we had a mutual friend who owned a garage. I used to stop there for petrol on the way to Melwood, and Bob would be in the office working out his horse-racing bets for the day. We'd always have a chat before training. So he never once had to wind me up.' But, chit-chat aside, the very idea that Souness needed motivating seems somewhat unlikely, as we have heard from numerous contributors, not least himself.

By the time of my second interview with Paisley, just before the Bruges European Cup final, his successes had brought him new stature in the game – the first two of his six Managers of the Year awards – but his modest demeanour was unchanged. He declined an offer of a fancy lunch out, preferring to chat over a cup of tea in his office, where he unspooled for over an hour about his beliefs, and his growing self-confidence.

'In their history, Liverpool have now won, or been runners-up in the league, FA Cup and European cups 36 times. And I've been involved in 26 of those occasions, as player, assistant manager or manager. The pressure of being at the top is much easier than being at the bottom. I couldn't watch end-of-season stuff all the year round from teams who aren't in contention. I couldn't stand that. I like the competitiveness of being at the top. Football for us is all about that. The aim is to win. All the frills can come after that, but they can't replace winning.'

His biggest test of management, he said, was keeping the players motivated as their experience grew, and they in turn became more self-assured. 'They're too old and wise for me to come in and tell them bedtime stories. Shanks would come in, set up the little figures on the tactics board, and say, "You're playing against a side with

Best, Charlton and Cruyff in their forward line," or whatever, and then he'd sweep the little figures off and put them in his pocket and he'd say, "That's their forward line gone, we don't have to worry about them." But you can't do that sort of thing any more, because the players would just laugh at you. So now I'm glad when someone – the press, another player or manager – has a go at us. I can use that. I'm always picking my brains at home to find something new, searching for the little straws.'

The psychological side of Paisley's preparations might have become more subtle at that time, but Liverpool's playing style was emphatically the same as it always was, irrespective of whichever new players had come into the team. 'The largest part of our game is still ball control, accurate passing and good movement. And it's also about patience, which demands intense concentration. We preach that to them day in, day out. People may say, "Oh, that's easy," but Geoff Boycotts are few and far between, and that's the level of concentration we're talking about. Basically, we're about good, sound passing and cutting out the chancy ball, which you sometimes have to try to create something. But we try and do four safe balls for every chancy one. And you can also make things happen by good movement. I can give you a negative pass, but I've then got to have a positive thought by making a positive run, so that you in turn don't have to give a negative pass. If someone's giving a negative pass, you shouldn't look at him but at what the other players are doing. The perfect player hasn't been born, so you have to ensure that you can cover people's weaknesses within the frame-work of the team. A player mustn't challenge individually. If you go in among four opponents, they'll destroy you. We pressurise collectively. The nearest man to the ball closes it down, but you wait for help to arrive, you mustn't go diving in.'

The evolution of that late 1970s-early 1980s team had a football-playing defence at its core. With Alan Hansen and Phil Thompson, and later Mark Lawrenson, Paisley deployed defenders who weren't the flat-foreheaded breed of his day, but bright, adventurous players who could spring from defence to attack.

'If you can win the ball by interception it not only cuts down on injuries (because the more physical contact the greater the chance of injury), but it also means you can use the ball better because you've got it cleanly, you're not at full stretch, and you're in space. We watch other teams to get their general formation but not to concentrate on individuals destructively. We've never set one man on another in midfield in all my time here. We prefer the zonal formation. Take [John] Robertson of Forest, who can run teams ragged: we contained him without even having a man marking him closely. And if you watch a goalkeeper take two kicks, you should be able after that to place a man within two yards of where the ball will land. If the opposition have a young, inexperienced player in their side, you don't go diving in on him, because he might beat you instinctively, and then he'll gain confidence. So you hang off from him and say, "All right, laddie, what are you going to do now?" Simple things like these may seem unimportant, yet they're so important to a game, it doesn't bear thinking about!'

If these words had come from one of the self-styled gurus of 1970s' English football – and you know the type I mean – they would probably have had other coaches and commentators gasping at the brilliant simplicity of their thought. But Bob Paisley never advertised himself or shouted the odds because that was not the Liverpool way. 'He always used to call himself just an old buffer,' Terry McDermott recalls, 'trying to play himself down. But you couldn't win what he did without earning respect, and nobody should ever try to take anything away from his record as a manager.'

Graeme Souness is in no doubt about the depth of Paisley's achievements, but it always bothered him why Paisley would constantly make small adjustments to the team, or bring in new players when he had a squad of strong-minded, self-motivating internationals who'd won Championships, European Cups and practically every trophy going by 1983. When Souness eventually became manager, he finally found the answer to what made the man he nicknamed 'Duggie Doin's' tick: 'When I was ten years down the road after Bob, I stood at his window at Melwood as manager, watching the boys training. He had a radiator just below the window and we used to joke about him warming his balls on it while we were out in the freezing cold. So there I am, standing over the same radiator, and one day I asked Tom Saunders – "Did Duggie ever realise what he had with that group of players of the late '70s and early '80s?" And Tom turned to me and said: "He was never happy. He always wanted to improve on what was there." That says it all about Liverpool under Bob Paisley. He was never satisfied, he would never settle for anything but the best.'

In 1983, the year Paisley announced his retirement, it was Souness who spontaneously offered him the chance to go up and collect the League Cup after Liverpool had beaten Manchester United at Wembley. 'I didn't need to ask twice,' Souness says with a grin. 'He was up there like a shot!' Thirty-three years on from the acute disappointment of being left out of a Cup final side, Paisley finally walked up the steps to the Royal Box and got his hands on a trophy at Wembley. And when he returned in August for the Charity Shield, Paisley paraded around the ground in a version of the Pope-mobile, hand in hand with his old team-mate Matt Busby, two great men of football, saying goodbye.

In 1993 I wrote again to Paisley, hoping for contributions to a feature I was writing for *The Observer* on the last days of Anfield's famous Kop. His wife Jessie sent me a note back, confirming the tragic news that Alzheimer's Disease had cruelly wiped away all memory of his great achievements.

But Bob Paisley lives on. Not only in the minds of those who joined him on the great journeys to Rome, Wembley and Paris, but also in the work of his many disciples who still espouse the virtues of dedication, integrity and simplicity that show the people's game at its very best.